Clipped Wing

No Flight Without The Right

by Robert Graham

Copyright 2018 Commline Publishing
All rights reserved
ISBN-10: 1727079744
ISBN-13: 978-1727079746

CONTENTS

Acknowledgements

The wave to encourage everyone to have a say in political and social issues has begun. Well, at least it has awoken the right wing from a thirty-year coma. People who have been spectators or disengaged from politics for their entire lives are now speaking up and having an opinion. People who view themselves as Centrists or those with even slightly economically responsible attitudes are now branded Alt Right and Far Right by the mainstream media.

I would like to acknowledge people who have had the courage to speak out against things they are concerned about in the Western World. Knowing they will experience severe backlash, harmful lies, marginalisation and risk to their own personal safety. People who speak their truth even if others don't agree.

I firmly believe that everyone has a right to their opinions and the right to communicate them. If someone is insane or corrupt, then let me hear them speak and I will be the judge of that. I am not so gullible or naïve that I need to be sheltered from future 'potential' Adolf Hitlers, by the 'friendly government' who has 'only our best interests' at heart. It is not the role of government to censor political opinions that differ from the mainstream, progressive movement and while in Australia our freedom of speech is somewhat restricted, we do have implied freedom of political speech which is protected by our Constitution.

I would like to acknowledge anyone to the right of Karl Marx who has come into the public eye for speaking their minds about political topics. They may have faced criticism, lies, verbal abuse and threats of physical violence. The extent of lying by the mainstream media has been astonishing this past year. They have set new lows and showed themselves to be part of the most powerful organised crime syndicate in the world. The great purge of the 21st Century has begun and with a bit of luck we will live in a democracy with freedom of speech again soon.

Preface

Australian politics has always been a fairly boring subject for me. I have always felt a bit disconnected from it. Like it doesn't really matter which party in the two-party-preferred system wins, eventually the other party will win again, and things will swing back and forth over time like a giant taking one step with the left leg and the next step with the right leg. The Australian public become mildly interested in politics every time the Prime Minister is thrown out or some sex scandal occurs and then we all go back to sleep again until some tidbit of gossip again dominates the media. People chit chat about politics every now and then at work or in cafes. But it is more shallow jokes about how useless the politicians are or how they don't deserve their retirement benefits. They are not talking about the actual politics, its more that they're whinging about how they don't understand it. Hardly the battle cry of a freedom fighter!

This gossiping is not a political conversation and the people who supposedly know the most about these details are often just repeating something they saw on the news and are often the ones who understand the least about the important subjects which are covered in this book. The world still seems to move in the same direction regardless of leadership changes, the national debt keeps increasing and we are constantly reminded about the horrors of climate change and how paying 15c for plastic shopping bags and shifting factories to China will somehow solve that. The direction the world is moving in is the real political topic for debate and discussion and this is where you will get a blank stare from the guy who was an expert on Barnaby Joyce's sex life five minutes ago.

Conspiracy theories and political activists have a place in the world. Whether their theories are outrageous or unbelievable there remains a place for your opinions, even if they are purely viewed as fiction or entertainment. Or maybe the way some people present their story is meant to be delivered in an artful, entertaining manner, designed to keep viewers subscribing and make you think as much as possible without losing your short, modern-day attention span. Maybe some of the conspiracies are just put out there because some information was made available by way of witnesses or insider leaked information warranted further research and one potential explanation was being theorised and posted? Maybe some theories are wrong? So what? A conspiracy is just a group of people plotting to break the law. What, you don't think that ever happens?

To use the law and a highly connected group of billionaires to silence such conspiracy theorists can only serve to validate the theories. If a lunatic was wondering around in his pyjamas claiming that he was kidnapped by mermaids, the most powerful people in the world would not even hear about it, let alone rally the largest, richest tech companies in the world to organise a campaign to silence him. But should this conspiracy theorist stumble onto a certain truth… well, how would a guilty group of billionaires with access to a Big Brother 'delete' button react?

Well, in 2018 they did react to a certain conspiracy theorist. This raised a major warning bell for me because all they could really pin on him was his use of the word "tranny" and the fact that hate speech is against their terms of service. This could justify perhaps removing that episode from air, but deleting the entire station? A multi-million-dollar income stream! So, why are they silencing him so urgently? In fact, aside from joking about transsexuals, all he really did was agree with the 45th president of the USA, that there was a network of people bypassing the democratic process and subversively controlling much of the US government. Hardly an extremist viewpoint and he had been saying it for years.

They never even clearly stated exactly why he was being banned or what was said that violated their terms of service. I am referring to Info Wars host, Alex Jones. By extension, hundreds of other conservative voices have also been blocked or erased by tech giants in late 2018 citing hate speech for perhaps using words like "tranny", or broadly suggesting that they are Russian agents, causing concern the Democrats are deliberately censoring conservatives to avoid the public debating subjects they know they cannot win.

Now, I don't care if you believe Alex Jones' theories or not and that is definitely not the point. I take many of his articles with a pinch of salt myself! A professional conspiracy theorist for over 25 years who had over 35,000 videos uploaded, is bound to have made some far-fetched claims throughout his career. The point is this: Does he have the right to say what he thinks? And probably more important: Do you have the right to hear it? Or are you so fragile that you need someone to filter the information which you are exposed to, ensuring you never read anything that someone else deems to be bad?

If he offers proof of his claims are you allowed to see such proof? Or should someone much wealthier and more powerful than you censor the whole lot for your own benefit? Does the government or a large group of companies have the right to deny me access to the information? Does Mark Zuckerberg decide what messages are right and wrong now? And will he use ambiguous words like "rhetoric" to define and enforce these new rules?

I am against the dangerous new trend of censorship and 100% for freedom of speech, excluding blatant defamation or speech inciting violence. These forms of speech were already illegal before the introduction of hate speech laws. If that means some people are offended by a rude person occasionally, then I suggest those few delicate people learn to handle social situations and deal with being offended. Your being occasionally offended is a price I am willing to pay for our democratic freedom. We live in a relatively free society, or at least we did up until recently.

We are not living in 1939 when 17 year old boys had to toughen up and fight to the death against Nazis. Being offended wasn't a legitimate reason for calling the police in the days when people had real problems and it isn't a legitimate reason now.

It is definitely not a good reason to dismantle democracy or restructure the world economy. If you are not sure what I'm talking about then that is good. Please keep reading.

Glossary

This list of quick reference political words is at the front of the book for you to browse through first. A significant number of people in Australia don't have a full understanding of at least one of these words. These summary definitions are sufficient to give you an understanding of the word. There is no better way to become bored with a subject than to not know what a word means. Half the reason politics and global economics can be so confusing and boring is that there are so many words involved which we rarely use in every day speech.

Capitalism
An economic system where private owners control trade and industry rather than the state.

Centrist
A person who identifies as neither left nor right wing as they may disagree with elements of both extremes. Generally speaking this person is either moderate left or moderate right but does not realize it yet, as they often lack any genuine understanding of politics.

Communism
The political and social system where the state owns everything, and resources and property are divided by the government according to needs and abilities.

Conservative
Favouring free enterprise, private ownership, and socially conservative ideas. Holding traditional values. In the West this is the Christian base. In the Middle East a Muslim would be referred to as conservative in that environment.

Conspiracy
Any plan made by a group of people to commit a crime.

Democrat
The left of the two major political parties in the USA. Usually concerned with progressive movements and equality. Leaning towards Socialism.

Democratic Capitalism
Capitalism with restrictions which are democratically imposed to prevent monopolies taking over and bypassing the democratic process.

Democratic Socialism
A political philosophy which aims to achieve socialistic goals within a democratic system.

Deep State
A group of people with sufficient power or influence that democratic processes can be bypassed to operate as a shadow government.

Establishment
The dominant or elite faction in a nation that holds power or authority.

Fascism
A system of government marked by centralized authority under a dictator.

Left Wing
The radical reforming, or socialist section of a political party or system. Far Left includes a desire for Communism and full government regulation and control.

Liberal
Willing to respect or accept behaviour or opinions different to one's own. This is a different word to the Australian "Liberal Party".

Libertarian
A person who respects free will. Libertarians seek to maximise political freedom and autonomy.

Marxism
The political and economic theories of Karl Marx. Essentially Communism and includes social reforms shaping the thought of the citizens toward Communism.

Moderate
Not extreme. Views that are slightly left or right and are relatively acceptable to the broader community.

Nationalist
A person who advocates political independence for a nation.

Neocon
Short for Neo conservative. The authoritarian right wing, as opposed to the conservative or libertarian right. Neocons are pro war and encourage expansion of the national interest through military means. These individuals are often a form of Christian or Jewish.

Polarise
The cause two separate groups to emerge with opposing ideas.

Populist
Seeking to represent the needs and interests of ordinary people, not special interest groups.

Protectionist
A policy of shielding local industry by taxing imports from countries with lower wages to equalise competition.

Republican
The right wing option of the two major political parties in the USA.   Supporters of a Republic support the right to democratically vote for a president, support a constitution and believe the law should be applied to all citizens with equality.

Right Wing
The conservative side of politics. The extreme version of this is referred to as the Far Right or Alt Right and includes the extreme views of tradition, including racial purity or strict adherence to the primary ideology in a country.

Socialism
The political and economic theory that states the means of production are owned or regulated by the community as a whole. The successful elements of the community are taxed to support the unsuccessful to create an equal standard of living for all.

Two-party-preferred system
A democratic system of government comprising two major parties and numerous minority parties. Typically, the system has one right-leaning major party and a left-leaning major party, allowing for democratic elections to balance the extremes of socialism and capitalism. Minority parties are forced to preference one of the major parties, narrowing the over-all options to two main parties.

Introduction

I don't feel wrong.

Does anybody feel wrong? I'm sure most people deep down feel as though their opinions are right, even when they know some others will disagree. If you knew you were wrong, surely you would work it out and adjust your viewpoint accordingly to become right. At least your version of what you feel is 'right'. I'm sure there was some aspect of your opinion which was right, even if you haven't yet worked out the optimum words to describe it.

Even when a person doesn't know much about a subject they will still have some sort of feeling about it, especially when it comes to social issues. So if we all think we're fundamentally right, why are so many people not agreeing with each other politically these days? How can everyone feel fundamentally right at the same time and yet not agree? Why the great divide between political extremes? Any extreme centralisation of power is flawed because of this basic concept. You always feel right, but so do they. So, if a small group of people gain too much power, they will insist that they are right, even if you feel that they are very wrong.

This book offers a brief overview of the main social and political factors influencing today's western world. These things affect you daily whether you're involved or not and you have opinions on them, whether you realise it or not. This is not a wordy book designed to make you feel inferior. This information can only empower you at whatever information level you are at right now. You do not need to study politics or philosophy before reading this book. I have given you definitions for words that are not used often in many circles at the front of the book to ensure you definitely understand the concepts I am discussing.

This book is not designed to be read by economics graduates, academics or philosophy students, though they would probably benefit from it the most. It is amazing how some of the highest educated people can be the dumbest in terms of political opinions and ideological conflicts. That is to say, dumb or very smart and corrupt. I have worded this book in a certain way to ensure my view is fully understood. Whatever the topic, I believe that if it can't be explained in basic terms then you don't know what you're talking about.

My intention is to get my message out to as many people as possible and encourage you to share your views with others. I am very interested in your opinions and want to make sure you are contributing your views to your corner of society. Because we are living in a democracy and <u>your opinion matters</u>. So, let's get back to basics and look at some of the main factors impacting on Australian politics today.

As I said in the preface, I have always found Australian politics to be very boring. So many people vote based on a general vibe of who they like at the last minute or based on loyalty. Because that is the way their family has always voted. Only Greenpeace supporters appear to be actively engaged and that's only because many of them think it is something to do with saving trees, smoking weed and hanging out with blonde girls. Almost everyone else is busy working when Greenies are out organizing and planning their activism, on a Tuesday morning.

You can actually hear people deciding who to vote for in the line at the ballot box. Many don't know the difference between federal and local government elections until the day they are standing in line. Most of us will choose between Liberal and Labor due to a two-party-preferred system. Labor supporters tend to be employees and have a union mindset, Liberal supporters are largely small business owners. A standard left vs right system set up by the mother country when Australia was first settled.

Lately, the budget is always blown regardless of who wins and so the national debt increases. We are told we can't have things we want and yet we always hear about tax-payers' money being wasted everywhere and it takes 15 road workers two months to install a path nobody ever intends walking on. Taxpayers' money is being allocated to Foreign Aid, U.N. contributions and Centrelink like it grows on trees but none of this ever seems to be an election issue as both parties will end up doing the same U.N. donations until it does become a major election issue. This frustration is the underlying attitude of a significant percentage of the voters. Add to this the fact that there is no clear left and right anymore and it is chaos, confusing and boring. Easy to see why so many people aren't interested. But is that all there is to politics?

No, it isn't!

Social issues are political issues. An interest in the areas you actually can understand and have some influence over will give you a starting point to grow up into a stronger interest and involvement in politics. So what are your views on today's social topics?

After reading this book I hope you will have more certainty on your views which will enable you to discuss them more freely and help to shape Australia into what you believe it should be. The biggest barrier to discussing these issues is uncertainty as that opens you up to being told you're wrong. Nobody wants to be proven wrong. So, if you are not sure of your viewpoint you may introvert and back away from discussion, which is not a good feeling and it negatively impacts on the democracy if a large portion of the population do this.

That is how thought control occurs and the only way to combat it is to decide on a position, look into it and know what you are talking about. Fear of being told you're wrong is probably the main reason people don't openly communicate with others. Not being sure of your opinion is a sure way to be told you are wrong when you do start to discuss things. So, the more you know, the more confident you are and the more you talk about it and the more feedback and counter debate you receive. The unsure ones are the ones who don't want to talk about it and are quick to rise to anger when the topic of politics comes up. There are no losers in a good debate, if it is done well. Step One is to know your facts. With certainty comes the calm confidence of knowing that you will not be easily contradicted.

The Power of Words

Just knowing the exact definitions of the specialised words in a subject gives you mental space to follow conversations and think and speak quickly with known concepts. This is true in any industry and you will see experts speaking to each other very efficiently because they will use specialised terms. On politics many people often don't have a 100% definition for words like Left wing, Right wing, Conservative, Progressive, Republican, Democrat, Liberal, Libertarian, Socialist, Communist, etc. This creates a situation where you don't have certainty on what people are saying and so cannot really reply to a comment without seeming uninformed.

Being uninformed is very common these days and it is considered polite to be agreeable and nice to everyone…yawn. To make matters worse it is now fashionable to be extremely agreeable with absolutely everything, so the unwritten modern social expectation is to stay silent if you don't agree with something. So often in today's world we are bombarded with information which is compressed into short bursts, so we don't bother to look up definitions of words to the level that people did say fifty or eighty years ago. Words are the tools used to communicate, both in giving and receiving communication. But they have another power. Words shape the way we think, too!

If you are someone who doesn't want to be called a racist, for example, then that desire to avoid conflict stops you from discussing "all racial issues" freely. Islam isn't even a race and yet many people are afraid to discuss it publicly because there are factors which are shaping the boundaries of your mental environment. Heaven forbid we should discuss immigration of Somalian Muslims or the fact that they are statistically linked to much higher crime rates.

Just the mere mention of those words almost causes a physical reaction. You feel wrong for reading them and I feel a little bit wrong for writing them. This is the result of mind control. You have been implanted with buttons and those buttons are now shaping your thoughts. We should be able to say and think words without feeling that they shouldn't be said. Words are not physical violence as many would have you believe. Assault is assault, words are just thoughts and ideas being transferred across space.

The mainstream media and agenda-driven politicians know this subject well, so they use word association artfully to steer your thoughts and shape your views. If we could objectively discuss sensitive issues out in the open we would be able to come to a reasonable solution. In an ideal democracy the government would then implement policies based on everyones' informed, intelligent attitudes.

For example:

Conversation #1
Bob sees something on Facebook, gets angry and the following conversation occurs:

Bob: "Islam should be banned"
Mainstream Media: Concerns over Increase in Racism and Alt Right Violence
Sam: "Don't be such a racist"
Bob: "Grumble grumble..."

Now Sam thinks Bob is a redneck, Bob decides everyone is an idiot and the situation sits there unresolved. He may even get more and more angry, have a few beers and then rant and rave and say something making him sound like an actual racist.

Conversation #2:

Bob: "Islam is a dangerous ideology, it should be banned"
John: "You can't ban a religion, mate. Freedom of speech is one of the things that united 1st world nations in WW2 and the freedom side won. There is something to be discussed here though. Recent immigration from 3rd world countries has increased sharply and more than ever before, also terrorism never used to be a thing when I was a kid and I'm not really comfortable seeing Aussies wearing the full body burqa, especially in banks, etc."
Bob: Fair enough. But what could be done about it?

The fact that John has already thought about the subject gears him towards looking at solutions. He is not entering this subject for the first time and parroting what the puppets on Channel Ten's "The Project" would say, like Sam did. He is not being baited into an inferior debate where he is nominated as being the racist before it begins. Sam's response is devoid of intelligent thought. It is stimulus-response and you don't even need a person present to predict his opinion on anything. You are having a conversation with a programmed parrot and the structure is tilted against you from the start. The conversation with Sam does not lead to any solutions.

If we succumb to the restrictions on free speech that are being promoted in 2018, then we lose the ability to have conversation #2. We lose the ability to discuss the subject at all and so no solution is ever agreed upon in the general environment. We lose the ability to risk saying the wrong thing, be corrected and learn from the experience or solidify our viewpoint. Our confidence shrinks as we do not feel informed and are reluctant to talk about anything that could offend someone. We only gain the ability to follow celebrity 'peers' who have scripted our opinions for us, like we are unthinking sheep waiting for our wise shepherd to guide us.

John: Well, I believe that an engaged public is what is required. A feeling of comradery amongst Australians or members of any nation. As long as we are divided in our primary allegiances we will have social problems. Islam is an ideology. But like all ideologies it only affects us if our own ideology and freedoms are challenged. As everyday Australians, our ideology is affected when we cower to minority groups and constantly change laws to avoid offending them. Like when Coles stops selling Easter eggs and sells Halal certified "chocolate eggs" during Easter to avoid offending Muslims, even though they don't buy Easter eggs. The real button that we need to talk about is anti-hate speech laws and the general concept that it is wrong to even slightly offend people. If that button were confronted and removed, then we would not really have a problem."

Bob: "But what about terrorism?"

John: "Terrorism hasn't actually been a huge problem in Australia like it has in Europe and the USA. I do believe recent increases in immigration from fundamentally different 3rd world nations has created an unnecessary problem though. This is because it leads to a confused culture, the formation of gangs and can bring global conflicts into our backyard, especially when federal crime statistics show a clear increase amongst certain communities." When people come here they should be joining our group and becoming part of it, not joining sub groups and feeling like foreign agents behind enemy lines and making our culture into just one of the many subcultures.

Conversation #3

Bob: "I'm not sure about this Gay marriage vote"
Sam: "Bigot"
Bob: "Honestly Sam, how am I even friends with you?"

Conversation #4

Bob: "I'm not sure about this Gay marriage vote"
John: "I'm against a politician being given the green light to change the Constitution. We filled out the surveys without even knowing exactly what changes were being proposed yet. Subtle changes could be used alongside anti-hate speech laws to destroy religion and free speech and marginalise the conservative viewpoint significantly."
Bob: "But gays shouldn't be allowed to have kids."
John: "They've been allowed to adopt for years Bob. That is not what is being surveyed here. I don't really care what gays do behind closed doors and they're not going to stop doing it to please you. It has been proven that gay conversion therapy doesn't work so what are you gunna do?"
Bob: "Yeah, fair enough. But I'm sick of seeing gay stuff everywhere, like in schools and they've even got kids getting sex changes now."
John: "The real problem is that it has become wrong to discuss the topic freely. Free speech is the important issue, people are labelled as bigots and shamed for discussing the topic at all. I don't really care if gays want to be able to formally commit to each other. We should all be able to discuss other elements of the LBGT movement, such as transsexual children as young as four though. I do agree that child sex changes is a very concerning trend and a sign that things have gone too far."

You see that the real underlying button is that we are being told what to think instead of being encouraged to think and speak freely. The Progressive ideology of the left just keeps pushing and telling you what you can and can't think. You are always wrong, and you always need to be ashamed of yourself and improve in some manner. The only way you can be a leader in the left is to go on the offensive and tell everyone else they are wrong when they say something even close to being politically incorrect. Christians and some other religions will be against any changes to traditional marriage, but everyone already knew that. Many of these older religions are not about to change any time soon. Discussing how to move forward on the Yes/No vote issue openly and maturely could have resulted in the proposed amendments being discussed and people being comfortable that certain religious protections would be included as it went through. Instead it became a name calling campaign, your tax money being spent on one side of the topic and you got blocked by 80% of your 'friends' on Facebook if you dared to ask a simple question about the Constitution.

Open discussion would have helped to avoid the sort of situation that people were concerned about such as Christian wedding cake shops being targeted by lesbians looking for discrimination suits and payouts. Further public discussion could include the other aspects of the LBGT agenda that seemed to try to slide through alongside the seemingly innocent gay marriage vote, such as the Safe-Schools programs, which includes the new gender theory being taught in American colleges.

This is the theory that there are fifty eight legitimate genders. Serious changes to paedophilia penalties and other highly progressive movements may be able to slip in alongside the LBGT movement. This movement originated in Democrat run California and Washington. I think these are the main areas of concern any informed person who voted NO actually had and I believe there is a reason the leaders of the left don't want us talking to each other in a sensible, respectable manner. They actually wanted the full package to move forward, not just the single issue of gay marriage. This was going to be their Trojan horse, their opportunity to shower us with progressive upgrades and new interpretations of what is considered hate speech and other ways to strategically chip away at our free speech and the essence of a traditional family unit. All to pave the way for the big picture programs being pushed through the U.N. which are covered throughout this book.

Racism and Equity

When I first heard that the definition of racism could only be applied to anyone other than a white person I thought, surely not! How could the definition of racism contain rules that apply to one race and not others? Isn't that exactly what racism is? That would make the definition of racism racist! Has anyone even read George Orwell's Animal Farm? But, in reality, I couldn't find a <u>dictionary</u> definition that did this. So, the people promoting this new idea have decided on a new definition for racism.

Other races have as much violence and slavery in their ancient history as Caucasians and yet many argue that people of various minority races cannot be considered racist against white people under any circumstances. Many nations, even today, have slavery and most foreign cultures are actually openly racist and yet this viewpoint that only white people can be racist remains common in Western society.

The Collins Dictionary contains the following definition for Racism:
Noun
1) The belief that races have distinctive cultural characteristics determined by hereditary factors and that this endows some races with an intrinsic superiority over others.
2) Abusive or aggressive behaviour towards members of another race on the basis of such a belief.

Intrinsic: *Adjective* of or relating to the essential nature of a thing; inherent.
C15 from late Latin intrinsecus from Latin, inwardly, from intra within & secus alongside. Related to Sequi to follow.
Inherent: existing as an inseparable part; intrinsic.

The concept that white people have "White Privilege" in western society is fairly new to the mainstream and so it has varying definitions. It appears to be a belief that people of a certain race have superior opportunity, ability and social status and that this is 'intrinsic' or 'inherent'. Whether it is true or not, this belief system satisfies the first definition of racism. So, the term "White Privilege" is actually a racist term, per the dictionary definition. Somebody needs to tell Facebook, because they seem to have a different understanding of words.

However, it goes further than this in that it also appears to justify abusive or aggressive behaviour towards white people and by extension Republicans (in the USA) or anyone who doesn't support socialism. Because capitalism is supposedly a white man construct, so now capitalism itself is somehow connected to white supremacy. This now appears to justify verbal and physical abuse in the street, if a white male should try to openly and respectfully discuss the topic or any social topic. It also promotes the idea of diversity quotas, the idea that white people should step aside to allow people of colour to have high paying jobs, regardless of potentially being better qualified for that job. This is more prominent in America as that is the source point of this racist ideology. These things are present in Australia too, especially in larger corporations and government. Diversity quotas regarding gender and race are a genuine thing now and this means white males are being routinely discriminated against to make way for minorities to be hired.

It calls into question the very fabric of our society. Is it right or wrong to inherit what our parents and families leave for us when they die? Do you actually own your money? Should the government own everything, including the average of the reputation of people associated with your gender or skin colour and give extra assistance to people in other minority groups to "help" them? That implies certain races and females are disadvantaged because of their identity, which is utterly sexist and racist. Enshrining this type of thing into law sounds like pretty aggressive communism to me. Maybe that is the underlying ideology here.

According to advocates of this ideology, any lessons that may be passed on through family and culture, such as confidence, ability to articulate ideas, personal drive, family friends and contacts and persistence on a given course are unfairly and disproportionately given to one race over another and the victors should be penalised accordingly. So, according to many, this should incur a penalty or a tax that holds the most successful race back, to allow others to catch up. Whether they are the best candidate to perform the task or not. See the problem?

It's a bit like saying; Usain Bolt is running very fast. Also, he is such and such skin colour. So, let's give all members of that race a two second penalty in the next Olympics, to level the playing field for other races. Or, maybe put weights on their legs to achieve equality of outcome. Even though the fastest runners probably train harder, have a massive culture base and peer base in athletics and they simply do run faster, for whatever reason. If you actually believe in equality, how could you single out one race to give help to without seeing that it is racist to tell that person they are disadvantaged?

Even if some members of society do need help you can't help those who didn't qualify by penalising the winners. Well, you can if you want to but it doesn't solve the problem you are trying to solve, which is to find out who runs fastest. That is one of the most fundamental laws of the universe. It just never works. Liken this to a company hiring a CEO: The aim should be, who can be the best CEO for this company and do the best job for the shareholders who are choosing to risk their money with you?

If you don't get the job it might not be because of race or gender, but because you were thinking about your alleged "disadvantage" throughout the interview and appeared introverted or needy or overly sensitive. Or maybe you just didn't get the job for another reason, much like all the white, male applicants who also didn't get the same job. You don't hear about them, why?

Well, firstly because the media doesn't put the spotlight on them. But largely because instead of complaining and protesting, they are out there applying for another job. How would you feel if you only got the job because you are black, gay, eskimo or a woman? Would you feel good about yourself sitting in the foyer waiting for the interview next to all the white guys who don't stand a chance regardless of their qualifications? Would you even want to work somewhere that gave you the job just because of your skin colour? That is literally what a diversity quota is!

Is it white supremacy to have the attitude of dusting yourself off and trying again if this attitude was embedded into you culturally by your parents? Does that culture form a part of the white privilege construct of society because white people (apparently) tend to do it more? Is it racist to have those good peer groups in the first place? Am I Hitler for wanting to do the best I can and want the best for my children? Are these "peer groups" one of the social assets that contribute to white people having so-called White Privilege?

Moving forward, should white people be expected to blatantly ignore their peers and stop attending university for a few decades to allow other races to catch up (but only in countries founded by white people) so that they can also have equal social confidence? It all gets pretty absurd if you debate this "very new" philosophy even lightly. That's why the left don't want to talk any more. They have gone into full tantrum mode and just want destruction. If my relatives and friends were reinforcing the idea that we were underdogs in a community full of racism every time I didn't win something, I could see how that could affect my overall attitude and demeanour and impact on future job interviews.

If I only got into college because my race allowed me to apply for special sponsorship even though I didn't have the required grades, I would probably feel like I had a disadvantage too when I failed that same college. Just because slavery was abolished in the

USA in 1865 under the 13th amendment (significantly opposed by the Democrats) doesn't mean that anyone ever agreed to a total social and racial radical reset and a Marxist redistribution of all assets, real and imagined. Inheritance, family assets, group networking and other cultural factors still remained in place, as they do in every country.

The argument is that "White Privilege exists" and people with the grassroots attitudes that lead to Marxism are eating it up. So, after ignoring the fact that the name and the idea is completely racist and establishing that it exists, you have the problem of how to handle it, or whether to handle it at all. When it comes to solving this so-called "problem" we enter the danger zone.

Their solution seems (unanimously, which is always suspicious) to be, rather than the underdog changing their mindset to adapt to overcome an environmental challenge such as employment opportunity, education, social respect, etc., it is necessary to change absolutely everyone else's mindset to make them carefully tread around the so-called "victim's" poor attitude, because it is their "supposedly inferior" race or gender that is limiting their ability. A common viewpoint amongst our left-leaning friends. This is a viewpoint that they very readily seem to agree on in terms of any proposed social reform movement. It is amazing how they all seem to have exactly the same viewpoint. Almost like they all watched the same TV show telling them what to think... because they did.

When the lefties call you names just don't take the bait! They are the racists and they are the sexists! They will argue that everyone else needs to change, not the person who's race or gender is statistically losing in some manner. Totally the opposite attitude of common-sense advocates and literally any species that exists in nature.

When Obama was president Morgan Freeman can be quoted in 2014 for saying: "Stop talking about it. I'm going to stop calling you a white man, and I'm going to ask you to stop calling me a black man". Sadly, Obama did not appear to take his advice on that occasion and the results of his eight years of constant racist rhetoric are not hard to find.

When discussing this topic with a socialist you will get the word "equity" being thrown around. It makes them feel smart to use a word that they heard someone important use. White people have more 'social equity' than other races (apparently). The funny thing is, the more you buy into this viewpoint the more you can make it true. It's a bit like reading star signs; you ignore the ones you don't feel apply to you and are shocked and amazed when they are applicable (despite the broad ambiguous language and the fact that the same star reading apparently applies to 1/12th of society).

Attitude is the way forward. It always has been, and it always will be. If a darker skinned person buys into the idea that he has lower social equity, she might pull a slightly disgruntled face expression or be slightly touchy about the price when buying a car. This causes her to negotiate poorly and aggressively. The dealer refuses to drop the price and so, it is all because of racism. Same dealer sells a car to a happy, polite white female who negotiates well, suddenly the price can be dropped. Well, that doesn't prove anything, other than the first person needs to work on their negotiation skills. Instead, she walks away crying about racism or sexism and thinks she has won the lotto when she tells her story to some creepy lawyer.

Here is the real experiment: White guy walks around being rude and obnoxious to people all day. Wearing his hoody up, smelling like last night's liquor, asking for cigarettes and spare change and pacing back and forth making unusual foreign hand gestures to his equally dodgy looking friends. Let's see all that white privilege flow towards him now. Didn't think so! Funnily enough many of the Hollywood American people I hear really pushing this concept of white privilege are proving every day that race and gender is not a real barrier by earning over a million bucks per week. This should completely negate their argument... should!

Multiculturalism

The term Multiculturalism appeared one day in the mainstream around the late '80s to early '90s. It came into the education system and mainstream media without discussion or debate. It was never an election issue, it just appeared. Reinforced over and over by mainstream media as being a great thing. I was in primary school at the time and we were constantly reminded that some Chinese people also came over and mined gold in the early days, almost as if we needed to be convinced or reminded that multiculturalism was always here… or re-educated! I have never needed to be reminded that water is wet. Truth has a funny way of being self-evident.

So, was multiculturalism always here and what does it actually mean? And where does that leave us as far as a national identity? It has a very different meaning to multiracial. Multiracial, would mean something like: People of all backgrounds living together under a common set of colour blind laws that are applied equally to all citizens, developing a mutual culture and respecting each other, all working towards the common good of the nation.

Multiculturalism seems to imply that people from all over the world can set up and connect to their existing subcultures in a different country, without any consideration toward developing and contributing to a mutual culture or working towards the survival of the nation as an independent entity. This encourages segregation and subcultures that may have conflicting attitudes towards larger scale political problem solving. They may even be at war with each other! They may be more loyal to a foreign entity than to Australia, yet they have equal rights, an equal voice and can vote the same number of times that you can in our elections.

In ancient Greece faith in Zeus was universal. Every culture has been built on a common basic religious viewpoint. With multiculturalism this common building block is nullified, almost as if by design. Social reform to make religion obsolete and make way for a new universal religion perhaps? How does a culture suddenly decide that it wants every single other culture to come and live within its borders alongside it? How could that decision to water itself down spontaneously come from within a culture? It's literally impossible; this idea must have come from a highly influential external source.

Some of these people might be from cultures where democracy was never established, so it would stand to reason that they may not have the grassroots attitudes and peer advice creating a culture towards protecting such freedom. The western world has become very slack in this regard due to so many years of having an amazing lifestyle and being distracted by spending our weekends drinking and buying bits of colourful plastic and watching television. Freedom that many of our relatives died to secure, while fighting not just against other nations but globally uniting with other likeminded nations against dangerous ideologies like communism, fascism and socialism. So, this "melting pot" is being made up of ingredients from all over the world, including the people we were defending ourselves against in previous wars. In fact, it is the first time this concept has ever been tried on this planet! What could possibly go wrong? How are so many media personalities so very certain that this is the correct way forward?

If it is to work, something would have to fill the void to unite everyone together as one. If the group has any chance of surviving as a nation, then some sort of overall philosophy would have to undercut the religions, without directly contradicting them and causing a civil war. Being encouraged to form a mutual group creates the overall group identity and makes each member realise they are a part of that group. They should, therefore, put the priorities of the group ahead of other outside interests that may have been social pillars of the nation they came from. Reinforcing and creating new social pillars and agreements toward a common goal; the survival and prosperity of this nation.

Cognitive Dissonance

To simply move to a new country without changing one's attitude and committing to joining that group would be to exist with cognitive dissonance.

Definition: *Noun. The state of having inconsistent thoughts, beliefs or attitudes, especially as relating to behavioural decisions and attitude change.*

Do you want the nation to thrive or would a part of you prefer it to fail? This either leaves you with anxiety, while sitting in indecision or it ultimately leads to making a choice. Where do my loyalties lie? You either choose to become a member of that country and work towards its survival, or overtly decide not to and promote destructive ideas. Deciding not to means primarily being a member of a different, external group who happens to be inside the borders of a foreign country. It opens the door to the possibility of being an enemy to the group, especially if the ideology you serve first and foremost promotes hatred and destruction of your new group. More so, if you perceive that your new home is responsible for destroying your old home.

Flying the flag of the Nation you join should be done with pride. Yet, flying the flag in any western country is now considered by some to be sending the wrong message, a message of racism. I believe that the intended message is "let's all fly the same flag and celebrate our nation as one proud group". If the objecting parties would see that and fly the same flag, it would cancel the whole flag issue and unite the country as a nation. Who would want us to stop being proud of our nation?

People who support socialism will often be opposed to "flying the flag" in western countries (actually they will often support flying every other flag but their own). This is because they are supposedly ashamed of their country for not instantly adopting the socialistic attitudes and other new age movements. Or perhaps because the western world is primarily capitalist and they are opposed to capitalism. Whatever the reason for their objection, it is perfectly acceptable to be opposed to something politically and discuss it with people openly; you have the right to discuss it and share your ideas freely.

That is called freedom of speech and it is important because it gives people the choice to join you or oppose you. If they oppose you, they do so with an informed attitude, which is fine. Who knows, they may even change your mind one day! If they don't hear you speak, there is a void in the public square and the laws of nature will ensure that this void is filled by some other idea. Maybe something far worse than anything that has ever been tried before (global socialism).

If you don't agree with me that's fine but don't silence me. Silencing me, such as supporting anti-hate speech laws, goes against the natural balance of a left and right wing. It rapidly shifts the Overton Window (see the next chapter) towards your views and makes it harder for people to talk objectively about all sides of a subject. Using laws to shut out the right wing viewpoint in media and in private life opens up a void further left of the most extreme leftists. The Overton Window shifts left but remains the same overall size, creating new space on the far left. What on Earth could reside any further left than the lunacy that we have on the extreme of that side now? We already have four-year-old transgender children, polygamists, trans-species, trans-race and paedophilia advocates. How much further toward the progressive left is it even possible to go?

It is hard enough for people to articulate their thoughts these days, with the erosion of vocabulary from the western culture and education system. Especially political and philosophical vocabulary. Something has occurred that ensures we are not engaging each other on these subjects. I think this is one of the main reasons for the divide. I see people trying to quickly summarise their thoughts because they have a two second window before the other guy's attention span expires or some childish triggering occurs and they storm off in a huff.

In attempting to summarise their support for border security, a strong economy, an aversion to terrorism and a general feeling of national pride, they make a broad statement that sounds racist. Or, they themselves get frustrated and their argument is very efficiently condensed into "F@#k you". This is caught on camera and you are permanently branded an "alt right racist" and the divide widens. If we could all just re-learn the subtle art of talking to each other politely like they used to do a few generations ago we might just get somewhere.

The Overton Window

When I use the term "Overton Window" I refer to the range of topics that are permissible for public discourse. Without causing a scene that is! Things that we should be able to discuss openly but can't (if you have an opinion different to the mainstream). Certain things start to fall outside the range of acceptable social discourse as the window shifts over time. Falling towards the outer edges of the window in Australia 2018 would be things like:

- The rights of men in divorce settlements.
- Aboriginal welfare.
- Immigration policy.
- Credibility of certain media stations.
- Anything including the word 'conspiracy'.
- White males having any level of pride.
- Climate change.
- LBGTQXYZ.
- Feminism. Jokes even slightly degrading women, etc.
- Religion.

These topics can be difficult to discuss without causing outrage if you don't agree with the more left-leaning viewpoint. Any objection or hint of disagreement can lead to varying social consequences. It is very common for people to lose their job for saying the wrong thing. Tapping into a wave of resentment and anger that had been brewing for decades, Donald Trump significantly yanked the Overton Window back towards the right and momentum is increasing to the point where free thought and open conversation is almost possible in the streets again. But these topics and many more had started to work their way towards the edge of the range of acceptable social discourse over at least the last 20-30 years.

Even now, when on topics like these it sometimes feels necessary to look over one's shoulder, as if you are discussing the location of your next Klan meeting. Even in family circles and with close friends it can be necessary to tread lightly on such topics, gradually hinting towards your common-sense viewpoint being sure to have all your facts right without being too blunt. This is the danger of silencing people. The Overton Window is given a perimeter by the anchoring points on either end of the spectrum. These anchoring points are the opinion leaders, the people who represent the more extreme or ideally more informed voice. To be an anchoring point and to represent the opposite end of a topic they have to exist in the Unthinkable end of the spectrum. If you silence one extreme but not the other, then the window shifts to the point where what was once sensible now appears the more radical end of the discussion.

It is not reasonable to expect everyone to be a fully informed expert. These leaders create space for others to exist within. That is why we need to absolutely 100% protect free speech even if we don't agree with everything a person says. It creates space for a subject to be discussed and joked about openly so we can build on our own basic thoughts and experiences and form opinions with certainty, not be handed a standardised, politically correct opinion that has been watered down, packaged up and processed by the mainstream media.

The Overton Window:

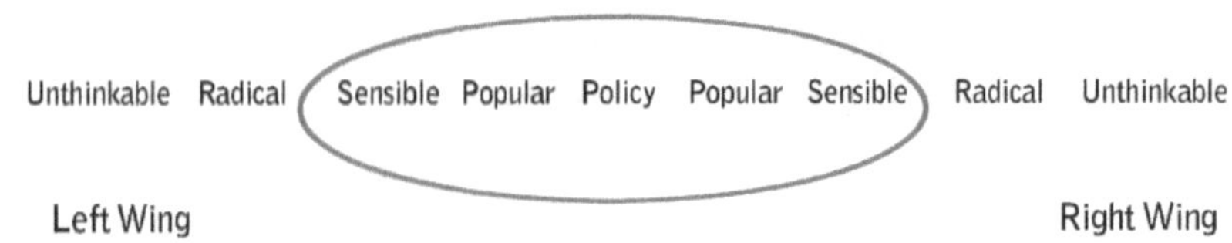

Customer: Waiter, waiter what is this fly doing in my soup?
Waiter: Well, it appears to be doing backstroke...

When this type of joke was first used in the 1920s it was considered unthinkable that a waiter would give you a sarcastic response to such a complaint. That is why it was funny. Stand-up comedians (decent ones) exist in the unthinkable realm because the essence of humour is the rejection of what is being said. It is funny because it is unthinkable, but with just enough truth that it works. Can we laugh at ourselves in 2018 or are we so easily offended that stand-up comedy can only be done now by minorities or people with speech impediments? The truth is, it is either funny or it isn't. I don't need a law to tell me if a joke is funny or not. If someone says a politically incorrect joke on television in 2018 they are censored and may be fined. Why? If it isn't funny, surely nobody will laugh. Does the law and therefore lawmakers dictate the direction of our culture, or should it be allowed to have an organic impetus?

If you were to take almost any of the above topics and earmark their location on the Window as it would have been, say, in the 1970s you would find that attitudes considered Unthinkable and Alt right today were fairly central ideas back then. Now, I'm not suggesting going backwards, I am simply commenting on how far left it has shifted over the past 50 years. Being gay back then resulted in prison; nobody I know wants to return us to the dark ages and it would be very sad to see anything like that come back in. It is important to note that we have shifted very far left and very quickly and such a fast swing in one direction can only result in a balancing out effect where it swings back slightly.

It is interesting to observe that the influence of Christianity over society has dropped parallel to this change in attitudes. The Window is where it is, the important thing is that we do not violate the balance by limiting free speech, which will cause it to keep shifting further one way or the other without giving the opposing side a fair chance to pull back and balance it. It should have a natural mid-point that can be worked out by people just talking to each other. Ideally it would be something that the media remains impartial on. But looking at the way things are today that seems pretty wishful thinking. Social reform is the new norm for the media viewpoint. What does it mean to reform something? To change the form of it? How much do they plan to change it? And will society still work when their changes have been made? Will we throw the baby out with the bath water and lose the lessons that previous generations installed in our culture? Who has the right to reform society? Is it even possible to create a viable artificial attitude of absolute tolerance over millions of years of evolution and instinct without serious consequences to mental health and well-being?

Since we are in a democracy; do we get to vote on these social changes, or do they just get pushed onto us by some all-knowing, superior entity? I have no problem with gay people being accepted into society and frankly I thought we were already there years ago. Recent social reforms that are being pushed go so much further than gay rights you have to wonder where they will end. The platform appears to attack everything that is Christianity. Topics like abortion, gay marriage, transsexual children, economic principles that go hand-in-hand with Christianity, like a strong work ethic and free market capitalism, etc. These are the things they are trying to reform. In other words; it looks like they want to delete Christianity from the western world completely, to make way for something else.

When ordinary Christianity becomes Radical you know the Overton Window has shifted quite far. When it is wrong to have the same moral values that most of our parents and grandparents had it enters new territory which could have unknown consequences. You don't have to be Christian to have basic Christian or conservative values, the building blocks and cornerstones are built into every level of Western society. Even atheists have some cultural connection to the moral pillars of society that carried us through the dark ages and two world wars.

Dismantling the family unit, encouraging adultery and promiscuity, drugs, prostitution, abortions, polygamy, even paedophilia, transsexual children, these are some of the things that come with these blunt, progressive social reforms. What does society get in return? All I can find is the implication of the unproven theory that we will be rewarded with a slightly lower probability that a transsexual person in an entirely unconvincing state of partial transition will commit suicide if we all change our attitudes drastically.

As a virtuous, liberated and progressive nation we will all be able to celebrate our proud, largely unemployed aboriginal people. Those peaceful nomadic people that we are not allowed to talk about any more. The ones who had no central government and were in a state of constant inter-tribal warfare before Captain Cook arrived. They wiped out an entire race of pygmies that lived here in earlier times, but we are supposed to feel guilty for supposedly 'invading' their land and building horrible capitalist things like farms, hospitals and houses, water filters and raising their life expectancy from something like 14 to 45. We can apologise and grovel daily for occupying their undeveloped land before the Chinese or the Dutch empires truly invaded and would have almost certainly wiped them off the face of the planet or enslaved them in the blink of an eye.

We can all enjoy the thrill of mystery dating, where we find out the birth gender of a person only after getting to third base. Because why would you even need to know? You're in love with the person not the gender right? What a great deal! If some of the above seems unreal to you then press your ear to the ground and speak to a uni student, a Greeny or any beta male who is dressed like a hipster with a neatly trimmed beard and girl hands. The leftist cultural Marxist movement is here. It is highly organised, and deeply entrenched in our society.

Hating Hate

ANTIFA has re-emerged in the USA. It is based on the concept of anti-fascism. But it is actually more of an anti-capitalism movement. They hate hate and intend to use force to fight it. So what is hate? What exactly do they mean by hate and fascism? Everyone hates hate. The sentence itself is logical. But without a definition for hate, it could mean anything. I hate it when crime hurts innocent people, for example, so I am guilty of hating something. Do they hate me now for hating crime? See how it gets out of hand?

The ideology is deeply flawed, and their stimulus response attitude can be directed easily by their leaders because they don't think for themselves. They are told what to think by their peers. They absolutely cannot debate unless they have full control over the platform.

Whenever I think of the Alt left in Australia the first face that comes to mind is Waleed Aly. We used to see him as more of a comedian/entertainer before I realised that The Project was a political program. It used to be a funny show. I haven't heard him tell a funny joke for years. He is actually a very highly qualified and trained guy and when he is not talking down to you on The Project he is writing for Fairfax media or rubbing shoulders with politicians at U.N. conferences.

Unfortunately, in Australia nearly all media personalities are geared towards either agreeing with Aly or not having honest or intelligent debate with him. If someone does start to make a point on his show he goes to an ad break or someone else tags in to rescue him. He believes that our economy is built on immigration, so any concept of immigration reform is immediately bounced back with "I hope you don't complain when we have a budget deficit". He has all the answers, because he is working for the guys that set it up that way.

He is an Alt Left commentator on the Australian version of 'The View'. He hates hate and he wants this human emotion banned. Any negativity towards Islam or concern over increases in immigration rates is completely unjustified in his opinion and it is his job to constantly remind us that what we are naturally feeling is wrong. Anti-bullying, anti-free speech, anti this, anti that. Everything in Australia needs to change right now to ensure that nobody is offended. He appears to be pro-democratic socialism, though I'm not sure if he openly admits this yet. His stern face lectures us on what is wrong with society and how we are all racist and wrong.

The truth about hate is there is a reason for it. Hate is just a person not liking something. Maybe their lack of articulation makes it difficult to understand their viewpoint, maybe they don't communicate well, maybe the media has framed things a certain way to polarise your thought and make it look like your opinion is "hatred". That is a reason for more discussion, not less. Never less discussion! Not restrictions to free speech.

The solution is always _more_ communication!

The basic attitude boils down to two main polar extremes. People who want government to have more power and people who want people to have more power. If you want government to have more power and people to have less freedom, then that is because you don't trust other people and that generally stems from the fact that you yourself are dishonest. It is a 'glass is half empty' attitude. If the media switched teams that pessimism and negativity would disappear in an instant. There is plenty of good news that goes unreported these days. The two sides of the same coin can be viewed in other ways:

Strengthen the government Vs Strengthen the people

More regulations Vs Less government interference

Reduce freedom of speech Vs Encourage open, free speech

Change everyones' viewpoint Vs Change your own viewpoint

Thought control Vs Free thought

Experimental theories Vs Proven systems

Shield people Vs Strengthen people

Ban bullying Vs Learn to deal with a bully

Drug everyone Vs Teach and model ideal social behaviour

Give a man a fish Vs Teach him to fish

The laws of nature favour the column on the right. There is a natural inclination towards strengthening yourself, your family and your group. If we do not follow that basic principle how naive would future generations become in relation to other nations that do not evolve in this manner? Even in ant colonies where individual ants don't have much freedom, they have a family mentality where other ants are treated differently to their own family. An inherent feeling of competition is built into every plant and animal.

They don't survive by sitting around feeling guilty and sharing their food with anyone and everyone. The lion doesn't sit around waiting for his food to die of old age before eating it. Equally, his prey evolves horns and fast legs or a fast, efficient reproductive cycle as a way to stay alive as an individual or as a species. Nothing is achieved in nature by sitting around complaining about injustice and waiting for some overlord to hand you your fair share, hoping he hasn't forgotten you all together.

The idea that we should leave politics to the experts is common amongst the left-leaning types, so is the uncanny idea that socialism could work. The left-leaning public would rather talk about entertainment or their own hobbies and when they are on the topic of politics it is always negative: "This guy is an idiot, I can't believe what that guy said". There is no "create" to counter their negativity on the subject of politics. If we don't keep one eye on our democracy we stop creating it and it will get swept away by the hard working, highly qualified socialist do-gooders.

Funnily enough their attitude towards crime and punishment is the opposite of what you would expect. You would think that hating hate and pushing for more government would make them want more prisons and longer sentences but that is more of a right-leaning sentiment. They are soft on crime and even agree with committing crime when it suits their political views. Border security, the same! The contradictions are baffling! All politicians are corrupt, they will say. As if it is just normal and nothing can be done about it. This allows them to continue on their course without having to bother with the irritating fact that their politicians are constantly getting caught breaking the law.

These guys cannot survive on their own. They could not function as an entire society without hard working moderate right wingers paying the bills. If they were all put on their own island today the place would look like Haiti in under a week. One flat tyre and they would establish a road sweeping initiative and ban the use of screws and nails instead of just changing the tyre. The power would go out and the toilets would stop flushing in under a week.

What Is A Nation?

The Google dictionary gives us this definition:

Noun. A group of people united by common descent, history, culture, or language, inhabiting a particular state or territory.

Wikipedia gives us this:
A Nation is a stable community of people, formed on the basis of a common language, territory, economic life, ethnicity or psychological make-up manifested in a common culture. A nation is distinct from a people and is more abstract and more overtly political than an ethnic group. It is a cultural political community that has become conscious of its autonomy, unity and particular interests.

Note: I usually caution against using Wikipedia as its accuracy of content and economy of language is not as rigorously tested as primary source materials often are but the definition is acceptable in this instance.

So, the definition actually seems to require that the people are united by a common culture. Without this is it even a nation? Or is it several smaller overlapping nations? No go zones are emerging in Europe, which could be viewed as borders emerging around nations within nations. When did we agree to dissolve the Australian nation and turn it into something new? A series of smaller nations all squeezed together in a new southern hemisphere Europe. I don't remember being consulted on that.

If you're genuinely not sure why a nation requires borders, then I am surprised that you've even read this far. You can support the concept of taking in refugees and even increasing immigration rates. Yet it still seems fairly obvious to most people that some kind of screening needs to be implemented to stop hordes of Pirates, Vikings or more realistically gangs, drug cartels, terrorist cells and kidnapping child sex slave traders from coming in and setting up shop. Yet the Democrats in America and their left wing, socialist followers around the globe are genuinely wanting 100% open borders and enormous increases in immigration from 2nd and 3rd world countries. In America the short term reason for wanting this is simple: they will all vote Democrat and once President Trump's term is up they will need every vote they can get to seize power again. They argue that it is inhumane to refuse to take in a refugee, at the time of this writing 15,000 people march on the Mexican border proving that weaknesses in border policy can easily be abused for political purposes. It is uncanny how CNN always seem to have camera men in position for a perfectly framed shot right as a smoke grenade is launched. Also uncanny is how the "refugees" travelled across Mexico from Honduras so quickly and just in time to be on the news during the mid-term elections when they were supposedly escaping persecution on foot, a physical impossibility.

This "open borders" attitude is reflected in the Australian Alt left and is equally confusing. In keeping with the theme of this writing, the mutual culture must be not only be preserved but also 'created' by all members. Not having a border goes against the definition of a nation and therefore adequately functioning border security is essential for a nation, otherwise it just isn't a nation. For a party to support open borders is a clear indication of corruption and that they will do anything to gain power, or that their allegiance has been given to another outside force. This has to go against the mutual culture and overall desire for survival of the nation.

Any party that advocates open borders or soft immigration policy should lose your vote on this basis alone, unless their members are willing to put their money where their mouth is and remove the deadlocks from the front doors. Article 61 of the Magna Carta, the founding document of Westminster law (Australian law), states that citizens have a duty of rebellion if the government of the day is ruling in a way that harms the country. I would argue that anyone advocating open borders is harming the country simply because a country, by definition, has to have borders.

What is the argument for open borders and increased immigration? Surely not everyone is completely insane. The truth is that most supporters are upset by the idea that we would turn away people asking for help and further, they soak up whatever the media tells them is right and wrong. They have grown up in such an easy environment they think this is reality for the whole world and they trust the mainstream media. They subscribe to the idea of maximising personal virtue ethics, they worship the principle of existing without ever hurting anyone verbally or physically, while turning a blind eye to other far worse injustices. This disconnection from reality can only exist in the most spoilt demographics of a wealthy, 1st world nation.

They do not realise how quickly an economy can change, as it did around 100 years ago and at various low points in the West's history. The cold harsh reality is that turning people away who aren't members of the group is exactly what a border is. My taxes paid for these facilities and my ancestors fought in wars to protect us from dangerous groups, crime syndicates and ideologies and created this nation for us. However, feel free to apply to become a member of our group, because we actually do offer you the right to join us.

It's the same reason we have locks on our doors, cars, pin codes on our phones, credit cards, etc. I believe that there is a way to help other countries without compromising ours in the process. It is best to go from strength to strength rather than risk undermining what we have built in the hope that it will all be ok in the long run. In Australia we have recently experienced a minor recession echoing our corner of the Global Financial Crisis (GFC), this should prove we are not immune to basic economic laws. How was it? Did you enjoy economic uncertainty? No, me neither!

What Is National Debt?

It is a loan in the form of investors buying bonds secured against the government that incur interest. It is basically a measure of how much people are willing to bet that the government will be able to pay them their interest on the bonds. So, when the nation spends more than it receives in taxes it issues treasury bonds and hopes investors, foreign and domestic, will buy them. If budget deficits occur and people stop buying bonds, that is when a nation has a real problem. Selling bonds also lowers the value of the national currency. Overall, I really don't see how it is any different to a personal debt.

Simplified scenario: Joe can't pay his bills one month so asks Helen for a loan with interest. Joe has a good reputation for repaying loans, so she lends it to him. Joe gets used to living beyond his income level and one day gets caught with a big unexpected bill. He racks up too many debts from his friends, then one day turns around and tells them he can't repay. Not only do people stop lending him money but now he has to consolidate his outgoings in a responsible manner because he simply can't have a deficit this month as he has no credit remaining anywhere, so he has to pay cash for everything. This means all optional expenses are off the table and he eats baked beans for the rest of the year.

When someone tells you it is more complex than that, know they either don't understand it and are parroting what a politician said on the news, or if a politician, they are trying to confuse you, so you won't think about it too much. I have even heard of national debt being referred to as a government spending tax income that hasn't been collected yet. The mind boggles! How is that any different to me saying my credit card debt is money I haven't earned yet? It just isn't!

On a global scale, some people won't even have the baked beans. The moral of the story is we all need to stop living above our means at all levels of society. Stop relying on national debt increasing every year. It is a bubble that will eventually burst, and it is no different to having a huge credit card debt. Would you sign up for monthly payments to some foreign charity if you had out of control personal credit card debt with difficulty just paying back the interest? Or would you prefer to get the debt under control first and then look at helping others after your family is secure?

Your nation is your family on a larger scale. I wonder how many of our treasury bonds are purchased by rich people in the same countries we just gave aid to? It is possible. I wonder if some of those investors who are willing to buy our bonds, could have been encouraged to invest in the country we just gave aid to. Now, using that logic; instead of giving direct aid we would only have to offer enough very targeted aid to create an investment incentive to people who have plenty of money to invest. Did anyone think of trying that yet?

To put this into perspective: Australians in 2018 are paying $1.358 Billion in interest per month on the national debt, that is $16.3 Billion per year. When you consider that roughly only half of us actually pay taxes this means the interest alone costed you personally around $1,300 for the year. That is just the interest portion of the taxes you paid. This money goes directly to the investors who purchased some treasury bonds. It is quite likely that this could be going directly into the pockets of a foreign billionaire. What would you have done with an extra $1,300 in your tax return this year? How many nuclear power plants could we have built this year with that money? Australia could have built a moon base for less than the interest we paid on national debt this year alone.

What is Socialism?

I think the bigger question is why do so many people always fall for it? It can be seen as the other side of the coin to capitalism. So the anti-capitalist is invariably drawn to socialism, whether they realise it or not. Pure capitalism comes with certain downsides including the fact it can leave many people poor and out in the cold. This could eventually lead to communism if large companies unite and get to the point where they own everything.

Pure socialism is often sold by pointing out the problems of capitalism, yet it too leads to people starving in the streets because the welfare structure lowers the incentive to work which erodes away at the forward thrust of the culture over time. Socialism is the concept of everyone getting their fair share, the government seizes from the rich and distributes to the poor.

If this were implemented today everyone would celebrate for about a month and then the economy would start to crash and burn. It has been tried at least fifty times in various different countries and always ends up with either total financial collapse or evolves into communism where people are forced to work in government owned factories to maintain a viable economy. Everyone gets an even share of nothing. The west has risen to the top of the globe for numerous reasons. Staying away from socialism is one of the primary building blocks that all western countries are built on.

Give A Man A Fish... A Christian principle on face value but the proverb existed before the bible, tracing back to ancient China. Whether it was passed on or perhaps a principle that was independently rediscovered and commonly agreed upon by various different successful cultures is not clear. The concept itself though is very clear and remains timeless and true. Give him a fish and he eats for a day or teach him to fish for himself and he feeds himself for a lifetime.

Ability is not gained through welfare and it never will be. Welfare has its place; the elderly, the handicapped, the unemployable. Temporary assistance for the unemployed to help them to find employment. A powerful economy gives you choices. A weak economy gives rich people the choices. Do you want to make choices based on your mutual culture and proven survival attitudes or do you want other cultures like Communist China or Saudi Arabia to make decisions for you? Obviously, you want the former, so reinforce the validity of your opinion by getting your nation winning and proving that your system works well. If your nation fails economically you won't have options, regardless of how virtuous you may feel about not having offended anyone today.

The nation survives and grows proving that your system is workable. Should some other group rise up and demonstrate that their system is better then take a look at what they did to get there and discuss it like adults to see if we can learn anything. It is not rational to want to tax them to compensate for your lack of production, yet that is what socialism would advocate. Capitalism cured poverty more times in human history than socialism ever did. This ever-increasing national debt is proof that the system isn't working long term and has been tainted by too much socialism. It is simply unsustainable and should be a major election issue every election.

Cambridge dictionary defines a do-gooder as someone who does things that they think will help other people, although the other people might not find their actions helpful. Urban Dictionary defines a do-gooder as an earnest but often naïve person (typically educated and white) who wants reform through philanthropic or egalitarian means. E.g. wealth redistribution, social justice, welfare, third world immigration, adoption of disadvantaged children, affirmative action and spending other people's money for good causes. In other words; a socialist lefty.

Do-gooders seem to mean well at face value but actually cause more harm than good. You can see that this is true because everyone they have ever tried to help appears to end up in worse condition ten years later. Teach a man to fish? No way! I'm going to take half of your fish and give them to him, then I am going to sign an agreement on your behalf making it law for you to give him a fish every day and make it illegal for you to speak out in objection to it. While you're out fishing he will probably break in to your house and rape your wife because he has nothing to do all day. But I will ensure that he does not get punished because he is disadvantaged and suffers from depression from being unemployed and unable to fish.

The do-gooder is easily manipulated, they hate the idea that someone thinks they are bad, so they make very poor leaders. They will always err on the side of looking like the good guy rather than making the responsible choice. The mainstream media machine employs a lot of do-gooders who appeal to other do-gooders. No mainstream media personalities like to make the tough decisions in life, they just want to criticise the guys who are making the tough choices. It is a very shallow and irresponsible way to live. Once we understand this fully we know to stop watching these puppets and start putting our attention on more worthwhile sources of information.

I am concerned that too many do-gooders have become influential in critical areas that affect the society as a whole. Furthermore, I am concerned that the rules are now tilted toward being a do-gooder, despite so much evidence that they are actually harmful to society.

What Do You Think?

More importantly, what are your views built on? Is your viewpoint built on stable foundations or on hearsay and rumours? A pyramid on a foundation of stone or a house of cards on windy day? The person with a more stable viewpoint will be comfortable discussing the topic with others regardless of their views. The person who acquired their viewpoint from the media or just imitated the general attitude of their peers will be uncomfortable talking about it in any detail and cannot tolerate open debate.

When Donald Trump won in 2016 it made people realise something. It made us aware of this entity called the Silent Majority. The nature of Facebook and social media is that people will often not "like" your comments if they are anything right of pure Marxism. This is because most people have a range of friends and there is always one pain in the arse in the family who will jump on you if you say something politically incorrect.

Many of us aren't equipped with time, motivation or the right debating skills to tackle this type of thing so many ordinary people will just read your meme or comment, smirk and move on without giving it the thumbs up or engaging you on the topic. They always vote for the same party anyway, so they feel that they don't need to think about politics too much. Add to this the fact that Facebook has adopted a world policy on hate speech, meaning that it applies to you, even if it isn't a law in your country and you get a total blanket ban on many conservative posts and more recently deletion of conservative channels altogether.

On the other hand, you have the university students on the left liking every virtue signalling pile of crap their 8000 "friends" post, which gives us the perception that there are far more of them than us. There aren't. We are just too busy working full time and raising families and most of us can't be bothered debating freedom of speech with a donkey. This modern social media platform is creating an environment where it can sometimes feel like we are the only ones thinking something is wrong, when we actually represent the powerful majority who built this place.

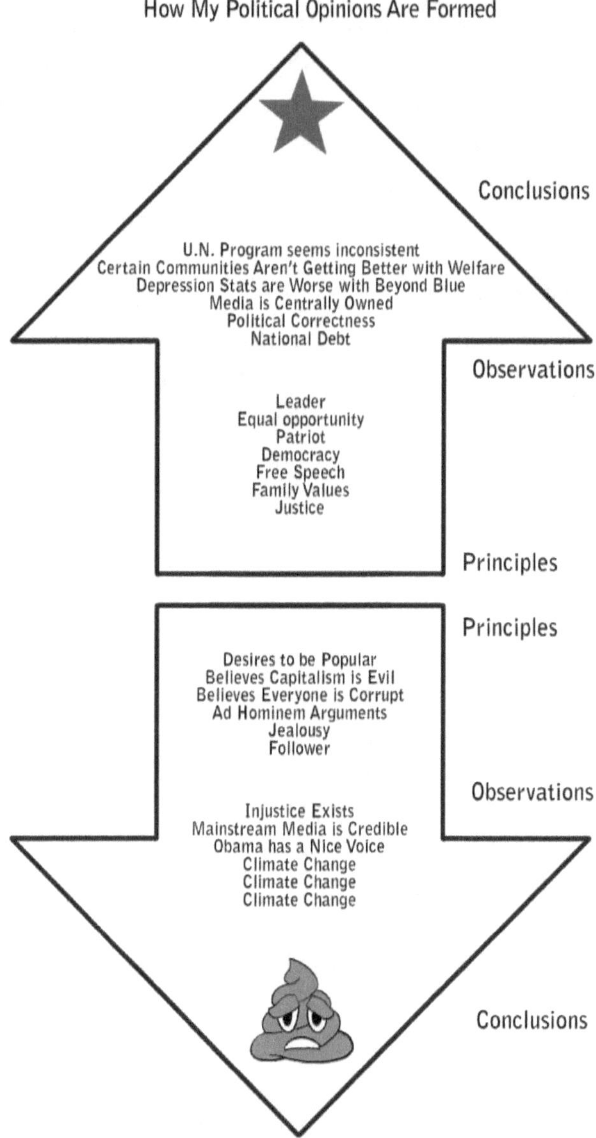

Do Whatever Floats Your Boat

As long as it doesn't sink mine!

Whether it's advocating gay marriage, declaring yourself to be non-binary and dying your hair blue, running a soup kitchen or worshipping Allah, I don't really care as long as you're not sinking my boat. What you do with your life and in your home is your business. I honestly feel that this statement fully represents the view of 99% of Australians. This is a Libertarian viewpoint, though that term is used more in America. Even the hardest right wingers in Australia don't want homosexuals to actually be executed, which is what occurs in more than just a few other countries. We don't even know real hatred in this country. We are so far from real hate that we label an innocent conversation as hate speech. The Overton Window has shifted so far left over the last thirty or so years that ordinary moderates (both left and right) are being labelled as far right. Anything less than radical socialism and total anti-Christian sentiment is now considered fascist.

Socialists can talk about the negatives of capitalism if they like. But as soon as it gets to seriously considering Universal Basic Income (UBI) when national debt is already spiralling out of control, I have to draw the line. University students can talk about being non-binary or skolio-sexual or one of the other fifty four political statements masquerading as genders if they like but as soon as they want schools to start teaching my six year old kids how to masturbate, which websites to visit for transsexual resources and making it an actual crime to address them by the wrong gender pronoun, I say enough is enough.

Feminists and those so personally and culturally degraded and introverted as to deem themselves racially or gender handicapped, can talk about racial bad gender equity and white male privilege as much as they like. They can discuss strategies to work together and improve their standing in the community through networking groups and education programs. However, as soon as we get legally enforceable diversity employment quotas in government jobs and large corporations, I know we are being lead astray by a pack of idiots.

Just discussing some of these topics in public could cause mass hysteria right now. This is how far it has gone, this is why the pendulum must now swing back to reality. I really don't care what you do, just as long as it doesn't completely undermine my national economy, values, personal security or freedom of speech.

This new age idea that words cause suicide and therefore free speech needs to be restricted, is pure toxic waste and a highway to communism. Many people lack the ability to articulate their views well, especially where politics is involved. A concern over mass immigration or terrorism can easily come out as a racial slur under the wrong circumstances. Especially with this new fad of everyone pretending to be offended over nothing. A habit of joking about your friend being a 'poof', can easily turn into a hate crime if you clumsily try that same joke in a different crowd in an effort to make them laugh. A person learning about politics needs to ask questions and discuss the topic before fully committing to a viewpoint.

Similarly, a person developing socially needs to experiment with conversation skills and make a few mistakes before finding the right balance and a natural place in the group. Being funny can be risky business nowadays. Joking about the parking skills of Asian women or asking a question about the role of a parent in childhood transgenderism lately, is like admitting you're a full blown Nazi.

If the 1,200 transgender people in Australia are so close to suicide that a question about the ethics of four year old children having sex changes will tip them over the edge, then I think they just weren't meant for this world. People need to discuss new progressive issues like this out in the open, without fear of being spat on or having their Facebook account locked or deleted for hate speech. I know loads of gay people who can't even keep up with the new rules that their own LBGT community are behind. From about 1993 onwards these laws were initially put in around the world to protect the gays and other minorities from legitimate abuse! At that time they made some sense and the laws went through completely unopposed.

Nobody was paying attention and people didn't see the significance of where it could lead. Twenty years ago we never expected to have these problems injected directly into our homes and primary schools yet here we are. You can't invent a new idea, identify as this new thing and then use existing laws to make everyone conform to it on the basis that you will commit suicide if they call you Sir instead of Zer. These hate speech laws were brought in before most of these genders existed. The truth is that hate speech laws shouldn't have been enshrined into law in the first place. Bullying, which is effectively what hate speech is, can be tackled at a social level without getting the law involved and there are already other laws protecting people from serious verbal assault and inciting violence.

Whether it's a dog trained to do a Nazi salute on YouTube or some guys doing a mock ISIS beheading using pillows, while protesting a shonky property development including a mosque being built to service 2000 Muslims in a community with only 37 actual Muslims (both real examples), the law is very clear on what not to do. You cannot offend anyone if you are a white conservative. Though, if you're white and advocating overthrowing the government in support of socialism, it seems that you can literally spit in the face of someone holding an Aussie flag in front of the police without consequence. Further, the police may give you an invoice for the time they had to spend keeping the peace because of your insistence on imparting your inconvenient views (another real example).

Unfortunately, minority groups are constantly raising the bar for what qualifies as offensive. Why is this? One reason is that the legal action results in huge payouts. There is a legal compensation mechanism in place encouraging minorities to whine as much as possible. Another is that social activist groups have formed, mainly amongst younger people, who reward this type of "social justice" behaviour. As if every complaint is a step towards a utopian society with pure equality and free 'all you can eat' lettuce sandwiches. Another is simply because we are allowing it. It is natural for some people to whine and complain rather than being stoic and getting on with life. But do we have to listen?

Apu being removed from the Simpsons will hopefully mark the end of a ridiculous era. When an Emmy award winning PG rated cartoon built entirely on all kinds of hilarious stereotypes, that is highly successful for almost thirty years, gets thrown under the politically correct, gender neutral bus, you know we have reached a milestone in political correctness gone mad.

When Starbucks, the most left-leaning corporation in America, gets accused of racism and resorts to actually giving out free coffee to black people, that's right, they actually gave away free coffee only to black people, that's when you know society has missed an exit on the freeway. When a five year old gets a sex change, well, being a father of four kids take it from me, we all know that the parents are really making the decisions in that scenario and the fact that companies and medical professionals are taking these people seriously is a major indication that we are a very confused society right now and even doctors have become too scared to offend anyone.

It's all just gone a bit too far and needs to stop right now and just saying that on a public platform could have your account deleted for breach of their hate speech policies. Comments like this are already being massively shut down by social media platforms. Accounts banned and permanently deleted even if you just spent $330,000 advertising with Facebook to set up your online business (another real example). That's the scary part!

Anti-Bullying Campaigns

Nobody wants to hear that a kid was bullied at school but it happens and it will always happen. It happened to me, it happens to everyone at some point, it happens to adults all the time. The bully is usually the kid who was bullied at some earlier point in time, maybe even by his or her parents and decided to reverse it. When you look back on it you think, if that happened today I would handle it differently. I would walk away, make a joke, try not to provoke him, worst case scenario even fight back and kick the kid where it hurts the most as a last resort.

Well, therein lies the problem and the solution. We simply aren't teaching each other how to handle it properly. In reality when I look back to high school I know that most of my confrontations would have been easy to avoid. Mums today will say "tell your teacher", "tell me, I'll go down there", "tell the principal". Today as adults we do the same thing; create hate speech laws, which is like encouraging people to run and dob the bully in. In reality, the kids who run to mummy get bullied ten times harder because now nobody respects them at all. The trick with any bully is to be cool and learn how to handle them with leadership skills, charisma, social skills and confidence. These things come naturally with being raised well but can be learned, too.

Imagine a non-binary (extreme feminist) stand-up comedian just laying it all out there warts and all and making people laugh with Zer (neither his nor her) incredible stories of self-discovery. That would do more for their radical movement than a set of restrictive hate speech laws. They would probably learn to laugh at themselves for a change too, which is always a good thing; people should always be able to laugh at themselves. Mind you, if they could do that they would probably get on with their lives instead of bothering to identify as a political statement masquerading as a new gender.

'Androgynous' is one of the fifty eight (soon to be) official genders. However, I'm sure you already knew that because everybody knows it is perfectly normal to be that way and being on the path to self-discovery should be celebrated. You will need to learn them all quite intimately if anti-hate speech laws and progressive movements are permitted to gain any more ground; and yes, your kids will be learning about them in schools soon, instead of wasting time on silly capitalist things like maths and science.

Problems like this are solved the same way all problems can be solved. Using a capitalistic mindset instead of the proven to fail socialistic mindset. Empower the kid getting bullied by educating him either with social skills/charisma or martial arts. Teach him how to make a few friends who will have his back. Dobbing to the principal is the ideological equivalent of asking for welfare when plenty of jobs are available and leads nowhere in the long run. That kid grows up to be a sensitive unemployable brat who can't handle an ordinary social environment and votes for the Greens. Actually, he will be bullied in that environment too.

Democratic Socialism

In 1945, the 1st world countries all basically agreed that capitalism with variant forms of Democracy was the best system. Not the only possible system but the best one that existed; and most importantly, had created nations capable of fighting off the Nazis. It was not a perfect system and capitalism always needs to be limited in some areas. For example, if it is left unchecked it has the potential to eventually evolve into one company owning everything, which of course, leads us back to communism. The degree that capitalism needs to be held back is the question. Inch by inch we add more and more social reforms, bureaucracy, foreign aid and welfare tilting more and more left (toward socialism). One great index to measure how the economy is going is the National Debt, which I spoke about earlier.

One ideology that has been brewing is Democratic Socialism, suddenly rearing its head again in the USA with the likes of Bernie Sanders. He maintains that it is different to socialism and just wants the state to impose heavier restrictions on big companies and share the wealth. But the true extent of government power remains undefined, so I really don't see how it wouldn't eventually lead to true socialism inch by inch, law by law.

Call it what you will but socialism has been tried and proven not to work dozens of times, often being democratically voted in and each time being sold as something different to start with. Sanders came across to the Democratic party in 2015 and with him the socialist signature concept of UBI (Universal Basic Income) started to be thrown around. The idea is old but with the Democrats behind it, it was being pushed through powerful mediums, the mainstream media, Facebook creator Mark Zuckerberg, Elon Musk and various celebrities all advocating the idea. With these mainstream channels supporting it and the word "Democratic" thrown in front, it is a tempting option for the uneducated beta males and virtue signalling females looking for nothing more than validation and agreement from their peer groups.

A closer analysis shows that UBI is not sustainable without a major budget deficit occurring every year. It was tried in Finland in 2017 and 'finnished' (pardon the pun) early 2018. You'll remember it was in Finland now that I made the pun joke! Two thousand unemployed people were randomly chosen to participate. The program was not expanded, and mainstream media were quick to retract initial statements that it had completely failed and that it "encouraged people to stay at home and play video games".

Charting the national debt of Finland around 2017 will not give any useful data as there were only 2,000 people in the test case so it would not affect that on any scale. Sweden, the poster child for successful socialism, is now entering a renaissance of right wing popularity with people protesting in the streets against the open borders policy and claiming the open borders combined with welfare and socialism is totally insane and guaranteed to go bankrupt. What's the matter, you didn't see that on the ABC?

Democratic Capitalism

Fundamentally this is what we have now. We have capitalism as an economic format and then we use democracy, a political format, to implement various welfare systems and donate government funds to things that are not solely economic decisions like domestic welfare, international aid, etc. The balance lies with the majority and how well they understand the fine balance between the principles of capitalism and socialism. Putting the word "democratic" there means that limits can be imposed on capitalism and that we can add or subtract these limits and make them an election issue if necessary. As I said earlier, raw capitalism will work but it has some pretty significant flaws, so I think the ability to add some restrictions is reasonable and necessary otherwise we would have sweat shops everywhere, a super-rich aristocratic class and no welfare at all, no minimum wage, etc. Basically India!

The key is for ordinary people to be aware when they are heading towards socialism. If we over-regulate capitalism, it automatically heads toward socialism. If you keep adding rules and regulations, then the format changes from capitalism into a system where the government imposes extra taxes and redistributes wealth and resources and so looks more like socialism. You don't have to formally rename it to change formats, it is a spectrum.

You follow this forward in time adding more and more restrictions and you will get the same drop in attitude that occurs with socialism. Nobody wants to strive to be the best because now the government has put a ceiling on it, successful people (or strategically selected groups of people) get taxed more and more, the unemployed can easily get welfare even if they are perfectly employable. Nobody wants to start a small business because they need five business degrees just to understand the insurance. It isn't worth saving much for your retirement because your pension is reduced if you do. So, they stay in their jobs and take no risks and from there it will lead to full socialism and then the government steps in to "help" dying industries by establishing new government-owned businesses and eventually you have full blown communism.

The power lies with us to either support or not support these gradual changes. So how can we set out a guideline for the ideal balance? How much should capitalism be reined in before it becomes self-destructive? One of the key indicators that I believe is important is national debt. If it starts to sky-rocket then the system is going bust. If the system is going bust, then we have too much of a lean towards socialism. Simple!

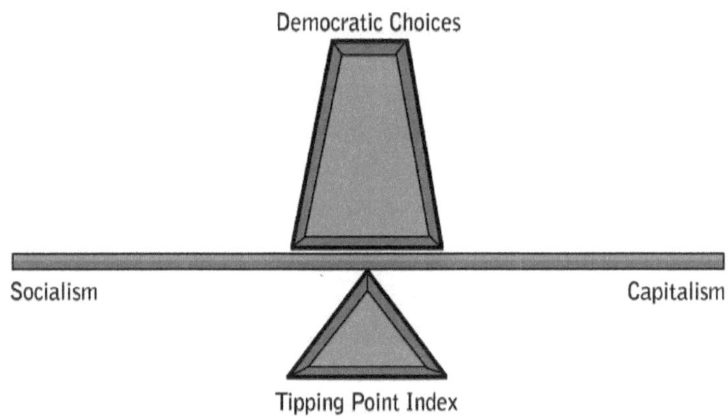

Now, if we lean too far to the left it is an indication that we are leaning further towards socialism. If we go too far past the tipping point, then the scale starts to get stuck on the tilt and automatically cascades further down in that direction. Again, I firmly believe that the main index of our position on the tipping point is the national debt. If the budget is in deficit at the end of every year, then national debt increases. If it is in surplus, then the national debt can be paid down, and treasury bonds can be bought back. We can do what we like with the surplus. At the time of writing this, the Australian national debt has increased approximately tenfold in the last ten years. America's national debt is around 20 trillion, up from around 10 trillion before Obama was voted in as president in 2008.

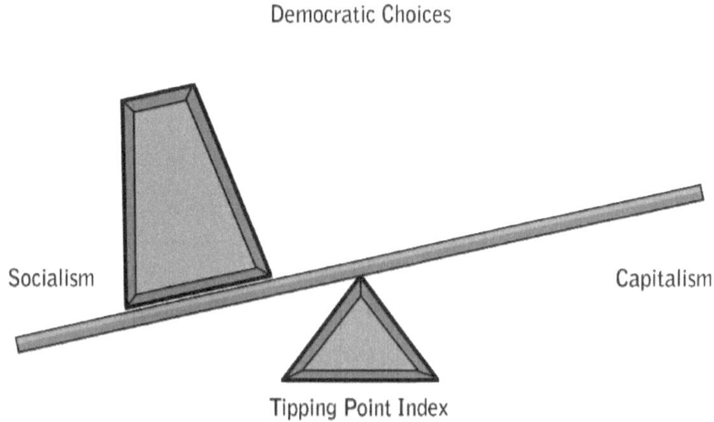

In other words, the last ten years has given the West a solid, almost irreversible push towards the left and this has put us on a collision course with a major economic problem. Interesting how increased national debt has occurred in all major western nations at the same time. Coincidence?

This appears to be deliberate but despite the conspiracy theories my attitude is simple. Do what you want with the budget surplus but don't give away money that we don't have. Ideally, we would use the surplus to further improve and secure the future of our nation. At least this balance ensures that we never get stuck too far over towards the left on this chart. If we are too aggressive with our budget surplus, then we would end up leaning toward pure capitalism and the various issues that come with that.

I would say that slightly to the right of the tipping point is the ideal balance, keeping a little aside for a rainy day. Surplus can be used in a charitable manner if that is what we decide to do with it but I would discourage foreign aid that does not have balanced principles connecting these nations to the international economy. For example, donating food or helping certain African villages to stabilise and succeed can actually cause a civil war if a neighbouring village was more powerful or influential prior to your help. Africa also has the other aspect of factions of Christianity and Islam fighting each other and warlords coming and going. Politically it is a highly unstable region.

The healthy, young, well fed teenagers of the village that you just helped, could now join a radical arm of a political faction, etc. You may even put a struggling supermarket out of business if you distribute aid too haphazardly. These are the risks with political instability and I think that is what should be established before anything else worthwhile can be done, without just adding fuel to the fire.

The interest that we pay on the Australian national debt is over a billion dollars a month. I believe we are promoting socialistic solutions to address poverty both at home and internationally. Regardless of how our foreign aid is spent, the interest on our national debt contributes to the deficit at the end of every year. It has gone way too far, and it is not an accident. By socialistic policies I mean welfare both national and international, people being given money without exchange being in place. Capitalistic policies are more pro-business and reduce regulations and restrictions, which allow businesses to flourish if people are willing to put in the work.

The new weight that can be added to the scale is the main reason that we have a national debt at all: U.N. donations. This is definitely a weight on the left side of the scale and it accounts for at least most of Australia's budget deficit. These donations are effectively part of an international treaty and often come without any positive return to the Australian economy. It is always easy to sell sympathy and make the theoretical argument to save a starving African child or to address climate change. But are we actually achieving anything? If so, why do the same nations still need more aid twenty years later? Are we artificially interfering in their social dynamics, contributing to the instability? Without political stability in those regions there is always going to be a demand for foreign aid.

Establishing political stability would be the first sensible step in helping any foreign group of people. After that they need to start producing enough food for themselves and then exporting something to connect with the existing lines of the worldwide market. At the very least they need to get back to basics and build more farms or mines like our first settlers did. Again you have the debate of socialism vs capitalism. By giving them a constant stream of aid it is effectively global welfare and it is a socialistic way of solving a problem. By setting them up instead with the capacity to help themselves and ensuring political stability you would be promoting a capitalist structure. I see it as being similar to the concept of helping employable people gain employment at home.

No wonder they need more help today than they did ten years ago or ten years before that. Socialism simply doesn't work. Every time I hear about foreign aid its 300 million here, 300 million there and all the while the national debt goes up by about 500 million per year. I'd prefer to see a budget surplus and a stable economy and political stability starting to emerge in the African nations. Maybe we can buy 300 million dollars of some product from them each year and assist their economy so that it is not built on the one-way flow of donations. Maybe our government can use the surplus to subsidise some farming equipment to help them get back to sufficient levels of food production. We could build the equipment in factories here and sell it to them for a great price. Some form of balanced system that generates production and an economy, not an artificial economy but a genuine one.

Dick Smith recently closed Dick Smith Foods Pty Ltd, an Australian company founded 19 years ago that sourced all of its produce from Australian farmers. In one example given in his letter to the other directors he stated that he could not compete with Aldi as the best price they could do on peanut butter was still double the price that Aldi were selling it for, as Aldi is sourcing everything from Argentina. You might say that is because the Argentinians are working for peanuts.

Well, most of the other countries have far lower minimum wages than ours (or no minimum wage) so, even if the currencies were valued equally, without some sort of protectionism the overseas products are always going to be cheaper, even when you add the cost of freight (not to mention the wasted resources and double handling involved in getting the products shipped here). It's basic economics and we have learnt that you can't rely on the consumer to be too highly principled and research everything they buy, always making an informed choice. I mean, how much time does anyone spend thinking about peanut butter? The government has a role to play here. This is a standard protectionism argument and Dick Smith has been making that kind of statement for as long as I can remember, ever since the late '80s, early '90s when everything became 'made in China'.

Dick Smith often argues that it is the consumer and the company directors who have to decide when enough is enough and start supporting Australian made products. But I don't feel that this is completely right. As if the directors are going to say to their shareholders, "Well, we made another loss this year because of our strict policy of buying Australian made products." How long would the investors hang around and how long would the CEO keep his or her (or Zer) job? Again, this type of thing is never a primary election issue because the mainstream media makes Dick Smith look like a far right activist and subliminally implies this by showing him agreeing with Pauline Hanson whenever he is in the news. Yet it is a major issue affecting the direction of the national debt levels.

If we were sourcing things from Australia each stage along the line we would be paying taxes to the Australian government which would significantly help to produce a budget surplus, not to mention helping local industry. We have made it impossible for certain industries to exist without being reliant on overseas products. With a decent education campaign the Australian public are willing to pay a little bit more for Aussie-made but not double.

Protectionism is often frowned upon but maybe it would have kept the Aussie car industry alive. A little bit in key industries is necessary to maintain a balanced economy, unless we remove the minimum wage, which often makes it impossible to compete. The overall index to look at to find the balance point for this is the unemployment rate and a balanced national debt. That is, it needs to be balanced at low unemployment and $0 debt. For example, you don't want to aggressively protect jobs if you have a huge labour shortage. Libertarians are against protectionism in general, but they are also against minimum wage, the two go hand-in-hand. So, unless we are prepared to change the rules in both of these areas, I feel that it is pointless being opposed to a little protectionism.

Without this the money is simply going to flow out and out and out of the country. The direction of flow is not sustainable if it is constantly pouring out without coming back in at roughly equal or greater levels. It all aligns to what appears to be a plan to destabilise the west by economic warfare making us completely reliant on China and other countries for various resources. Right now we mine iron ore, then ship it away to China to be made into a car, then buy it back.

If a person were to attempt to make the argument that fossil fuels cause Climate Change, then the first thing they could point to as a remedy would be that we should minimise unnecessary transport by encouraging greater protectionism in resource rich nations. To me, the fact that this type of thing is never discussed in the mainstream is an indication that the U.N. is more interested in positioning itself as a world government than in actually reducing the use of fossil fuels. It is up to the free citizens to take some responsibility for our government and stop these forces that are tipping the balance out of a stable political structure. The other side of the coin is too much capitalism, where companies have too much power and start to use their power unethically to influence politics and limit freedom. This kind of corruption has to be limited by the people in the democracy paying attention.

Funnily enough, the wealthiest capitalists are the ones behind the new push for western socialism. Google, YouTube, Apple and Facebook are the modern-day tech giants and combined with the establishment old money oil trillionaires, the Federal Reserve bank, the mainstream mafia, pardon me "media", and world arms dealers and a blatant push by the U.N. to implement greater controls over economic markets and you have an incredibly powerful group or groups that can influence all areas of the economy. So, they utterly abuse capitalism and then manipulate their followers to refer to their own example of unethical behaviour, to prove that capitalism is flawed and implement socialism with them being in a position to be the most influential people in the new government. Nice!

Where we went wrong in Western society was by not regulating the influence of these super rich over governments enough. It is not necessary to install socialism to impose these regulations. Just laws and other ways to protect and monitor the essence of our democracy will be sufficient. Banning all political donations are an example of the type of area that could be worth discussing.

This is a debatable topic but I believe that politicians should all be given equal opportunity to convey their messages to the public and then we vote from there. It should not be necessary to raise hundreds of millions of dollars just to run massive ad campaigns to be capable of winning an election. It should not be possible for a rich person to have more influence than any other citizen with an equal vote, that's why citizens each have votes of equal value.

It creates the potential for a conflict of interests. Donors may expect favours after their politician wins and politicians may be forced to choose between losing and compromising their integrity. If they don't directly expect favours, there is still the potential threat of not donating next time if they are not satisfied with an outcome or pulling donations if a certain topic comes to the front of a campaign. I also feel that it forces politicians into the position of asking for money which binds them toward the more powerful corporations, exactly the type of thing that leads to globalism. Government should be separate from industry. Your vote is equal to everyone else's. I wonder if Labor would remain so closely tied to the unions if half of their funding was not derived directly from them.

The Left, The Right and The Centrist

The media will often refer to anyone slightly right of centre as alt right or far right. This is to give the impression that two extremes are facing off against each other. They will rarely refer to centrists or moderate right wingers without labelling them the far right. On face value and without looking into it much, the left wing viewpoint will definitely appear to be more palatable, especially for atheists as Christianity is considered conservative and therefore right wing. When the media does this, they want you to think of a right winger and decide you are definitely not one of those old-fashioned extremists who were against gay marriage or the racist bogan looking guy with a flag in one hand and a beer in the other. This inability to identify with the right wing is easy to fall into for many people, especially with how the media portrays the right wing.

The media uses word association to implant underlying concepts into your mind. They have become very good at it. They can ask one question and that question can contain multiple implications and word association so that different people will hear different questions. A question about border security will now trigger a lefty, he or she will now think you are talking about genocide. Wearing a red hat is now the same as a Nazi salute to a small group of far left (ANTIFA). They will also use the word "rhetoric". "Look at the rhetoric, what you're saying is alt right rhetoric." But all you've really said is something like:

"Should nations have borders?"
"Is the additional welfare actually helping certain communities?"
"Should we screen refugees to see if they are criminals or have serious diseases before allowing them to live here?"
"Are there any biological differences between men and women?"
"Is non-binary a gender or a political stance on gender roles?"
"Should 4 year old kids be allowed to have sex changes?"
"Is white privilege a racist concept?"

"Did people vote for Obama just because he is black?"
"Is it ok to be white?"

ALT RIGHT RHETORIC!!!

"Rhetoric" itself is a word that is used deceptively by the media.

It means: Language used to have a persuasive or impressive effect, but which is often regarded as lacking sincerity or meaningful content.

It is the magical word that allows people to summarise what you are trying to say for you, based on how they perceive your theme. So, it is associated with their impression of you, not necessarily your true intention or actual words. With the average lemming or SJW (Social Justice Warrior) nowadays having the attention span of a puppy dog, they are not going to take long to label you "bigot" and see everything through that lens from that point on. It also makes it very hard to use exact language, which is now interpreted as subjective, rather than words having exact dictionary definitions, such as their with new meaning for what constitutes racism. Something can be deemed "racist" then you flip the words black and white around and suddenly it does not violate the Twitter "terms of use" any more.

So, a person makes a meaningful and genuine statement or asks an innocent and sensible question and the media or SJW deliberately labels it as alt right rhetoric. A Social Justice Warrior is a person who promotes progressive views and in recent times they have become capable of having students kicked out of universities, banned from certain groups, sacked from jobs, etc. People are utterly afraid of them. They claim to own the rights to the word 'love' and accuse anyone who doesn't agree with them of being a 'hater'.

Like a spider inviting you into it's web, they set up the framework of the conversation so that you have lost the debate before the conversation even begins. It is not possible to talk to them as an equal, because they are lecturing you. If you don't agree instantly you are a racist, you are hateful, a bigot, a fascist. Basic economics is meaningless to them, words now have ambiguous meanings. They have often been praised by a peer, such as a professor or a politician. They or their peer may have been invited to a U.N. function.

They do not need your advice or input. They are the modern-day zealot of a new age religion called atheist communism and they are enlightening you. Instead of responding to what was actually said they are now responding to what they are pretending you said, or how they feel about you or your identity or what they think that type of speech could imply or evolve into. They are responding to the "rhetoric" and so they are talking to ordinary family men and people who are proud of their country as though they are alt right racists. You have been painted with red paint and now they just can't see anything else. You don't use the same type of PC language, so they go into attack mode.

In western countries alt right or far right basically means white supremacist, but in a middle eastern country it would mean a hardcore Muslim. So, it has different meaning depending on the location. It means alternative right wing and the definition is vague enough it can now be loosely thrown around at anyone suggesting anything even moderately economically sensible. The media will always label anyone saying anything that contradicts the mainstream narrative as "alt right". That is to say, the U.N. narrative. They have whipped that dead horse so thoroughly now that it is losing its power. Most people are fairly central, of course they are, that is the definition of 'most people'. The extremes are far right and far left but most people are in the central region, centre right or centre left.

To see the media paint normal, responsible, hard working parents and Christians as alt right is truly taking word association to the next level, especially when they are so often not even Caucasians in the crowd that is being labelled white-supremacist. Instead of saying proud nationalist, they say white nationalist. They will say pro-hate speech instead of supporter of free speech. Instead of saying right wing they say alt right or far right to make it sound like a bad thing, when really; right wing is roughly half of the population. Logic would dictate that roughly half of the population is going to be right of centre, because obviously right and left are the two extremes and society always sits at the average mid-section of this. Centre by definition is the mid-point between left and right. This tarring of the right wing is a tarring of roughly half the population! That doesn't sound very democratic to me.

The alt left is the extreme Greenpeace supporting socialist. The moderate left wing or centre left is the mainstream population, heavily influenced by alt left media. Many right wingers are employed full time and are too busy or disinterested to be overly involved in politics or to explain basic economics to teenagers. So, we haven't heard from this side so much over the last 30 years. They have been tactically silenced by the left and many have become disengaged from politics, often feeling that nothing will ever change or that nobody is listening. This is what needs to stop. The moderate right need to get back in the game and start having an opinion again.

The actual far right is terrible and has been bad over the history of the western world. All 300 members of the KKK should be very ashamed of themselves. That extreme minority has very little to do with the right wing though. Actual racism has no place in Australia or in any democracy. There is a big difference between nationalism and white nationalism. The fact is undisputable that a person can look Asian or African and be Aussie at heart and that person is Aussie as far as I'm concerned.

The centrists are in the middle and you have moderate left and moderate right just slightly off centre. They are all supposed to see extremes on both ends as abhorrent. But recently the entire left half is behaving more like alt left. That is the whole reason the two-party-preferred system is so great. If the society starts to go too far one way, the other side kicks up a fuss and balances it out.

The danger of identifying with centrism is that it has no solid definition, so it can be easily hijacked and votes are dispersed. Before being deposed Malcom Turnbull, for example, attempted to identify as a centrist in a ludicrous attempt to make everyone happy and claim a central, reasonable position. The media started to say things like "The right wing faction of the Labor party is saying such and such…". As if each party has left and right factions. What a load of garbage, deliberately designed to confuse you, there is no right wing faction of the Labor party and there never has been. The Liberal party is supposed to represent the moderate right wing, not centrism. Somehow it has veered left, I believe this is due to an imbalance in right wing media representation and this tightening of media regulations in respect to hate speech which seems to have affected the right wing media more than the left over time.

The truth is that centrists are just individuals with opinions that range and move with the times and that is how a normal democracy should be. The average informed centrist can discuss politics without collapsing into a gasping heap on the floor. Sometimes a centrist will be able to question left wing opinions without necessarily being racist, prejudiced or a Nazi. But the centrists are not organised so there are no agreed upon principles and they get caught up debating with each other with no tangible product being produced at the end of it. Ultimately, I don't believe that centrists really exist as they are going to be more left or right-leaning, so that makes them moderates, even if they change sides frequently.

Actually, this is part of the reason that the right has dispersed so easily. 99% of us are not racists and don't want to be tarred with the same brush as the hardcore redneck that actually is a racist. The assumption that we all agree on everything is madness and that principle of total agreement is actually a mind control channel put there by the mainstream media designed to keep you central and complaint. This is why the Globalists have a very tight and seemingly reasonable ideology that is quite organised and consistent amongst their members. Informed patriots, on the other hand, can debate openly and disagree on topics because informed adults aren't primarily interested in following or fitting in with their peers. The left wingers are younger, on average, than the vast number of right wingers, so social dynamics and hierarchical social structures are more important to them.

This higher likelihood to disagree with each other means that we often keep quiet when we are not in the mood for an intense, open debate. Under a very far right wing government, like Saudi Arabia, for example, I would find myself leaning quite far left, if I could avoid being executed long enough to vote. This idea of centrism is the idea that you fit in the middle because you don't fully agree with far right (or left) wing ideology. So, as soon as you don't agree with someone who is openly on the right, you may choose to identify as a centrist, because you don't want people calling you racist. It's an uninformed position built in a factory called the mainstream media.

The Two-Party-Preferred System

This is a system of government that warrants a separate book and many have been written on the subject. Just this topic alone delves deeply into philosophy, western history, human nature, economics and politics. It is varying versions of this system that we have in the western world. The Australian system comes from our settlement by the United Kingdom and the early American system was also built on the same two-wing system. It allows for balance over time because both extremes are represented. In a two-party-preferred system both extremes are able to have a say and implement the bigger political topics with each wing having their time in the spotlight. The society reaches a natural balance in the middle of the two extremes which represent natural human leanings. Topics that are not agreed upon become the points of discussion and debate.

It includes people from all backgrounds and ideologies and stops the society from changing too rapidly under a radical, central culture and leaving groups behind. Media (newspapers at the time) were also originally designed to be split into two groups, left-leaning and right-leaning. This is the critical element that allows for progress but maintains balance. The system is built on the concept of balance through time, rather than being static it allows for period of left-leaning and then a swing back toward right-leaning to adjust and so on.

Right wingers have their opinion leaders and left wingers have theirs. Debates are had and reforms are discussed out in the open, by informed people and their followers. Not everyone has time to be an expert in politics, so it is necessary to get your summary from knowledgeable sources, rather than always going directly to the source yourself. That is the true role of the media and journalists in general. Commentators are supposed to be biased and journalists should be presenting facts only. The personal leaning of those identifying as journalists, or the leaning of their employer should not be apparent.

At some point in Australian history (and simultaneously across all of western society) this well balanced, two-party system became violated. Credible right wing media became more and more difficult to find and any opinion leader in the community who made any sense was labelled far right and shunned by the mainstream and the entertainment industry. Right wing commentators and journalists will usually at some point in their career make a mildly controversial joke and be sacked for it, resulting in a thinning out of the right side of media.

The mainstream had suddenly decided to become alt left while pretending to be central, non-biased journalists. I think this subtle shift started to occur somewhere around the late '80s to early '90s. Since then, many left-leaning people don't even know what left and right means and they just see everyone as being some shade of left, or a Nazi. The rules changed with the introduction of the term 'Political Correctness' and the various media regulations designed to kerb hate speech and opinion leaders inciting violence. It now gradually became unpopular to be a gruff, obnoxious right winger. In other words, it became wrong to be any normal bloke without professional media training.

Rupert Murdoch was born in Melbourne in 1931 but became an American citizen in 1985. Even looking very briefly at the main career highlights in his biography it is hard not to draw parallels with his massive corporate expansion and acquisition of major media outlets and the sudden shift of western media in a very organised and highly targeted direction. Conspiracy theories aside, the basic violation that has occurred here is that there came a point in time where the right wing was no longer equally represented in media and so the balance was lost.

The wing was clipped. The Liberal party (supposedly right wing) then gradually shifted further and further left until moderates and conservatives within the party were labelled far right and the entire two-party system started to look more like a one-party state where it made no real difference who you voted for, because both sides were actually left. People on the street lost interest and you started hearing them say "what difference does it make anyway?" When Prime Minister Malcom Turnbull openly said he was a centrist not one person flinched. The concept of the left and right wing had been almost completely erased from our culture and just using the term "right wing" had become tantamount to admitting you're a Nazi, which is really showing peoples' ignorance as the Nazis originated from the Far left.

This apathetic outlook is the natural by-product of violating the harmony and organic balance of the two-party system. Many people no longer felt represented, some were driven to vote for minority far right representatives in an attempt to restore balance or halt the sprint towards full blown socialism that so many were concerned about. The middle still voted Liberal but didn't complain when it shifted into leftist policies. This split the conservative vote and tricked natural right wingers in to supporting left wing ideas including slowly marching into globalism. This heavily manipulated, synthetic environment produced the most left wing Liberal party that has ever existed.

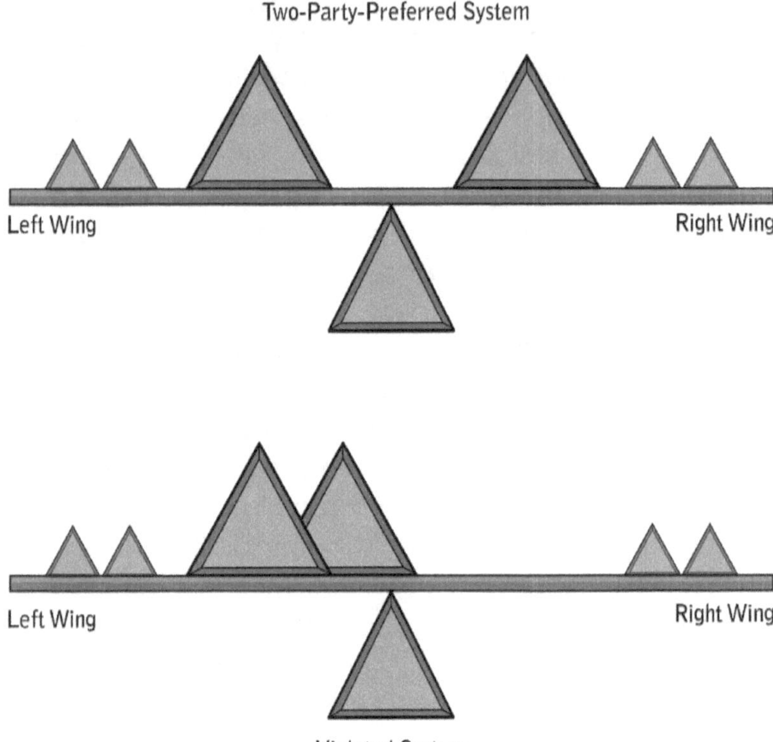

Two-Party-Preferred System
Left Wing
Right Wing
Left Wing
Right Wing
Violated System

This is the main reason that we have recently been subjected to a new Prime minister every twenty five minutes and massive increases in national debt levels. The right wing party needs to be at least slightly right wing for the two-party-preferred system to actually work. If society wants to vote left at a certain point in time, we have Labor in power for a few years. Simple!

Minority Parties are often necessary to form a majority in the senate and some minor parties are larger than others, but I have kept the theme simplified here. To be left or right wing is personal choice and both have been necessary throughout our history to make this country great, but to go against the essence of the two-party-preferred system is to throw out everything that we have gained as a modern society and go back in time politically to a time when monarchies ruled the land unopposed. A one-party state. That is treasonous. If there are polarising arguments occurring in the public arena, it is only natural for the right and left wings to take up appropriate positions on either side of that topic. The system becomes violated when both major parties take one side of an argument or implement a new law on any major topic, where the public view is a 50/50 split. It means one half of society is not being represented by any major party.

It can also be violated by one side controlling or managing the opposition of the opposite media. Many would argue that left and right are equally represented and that the right are just not as good. Maybe it just is harder to be politically correct when you are right wing in an industry where you make one politically incorrect mistake and you're fired. Many supposedly right wing media outlets still support climate change action and U.N. funding, generally the same ones that advocate war. Complete freedom and independence in journalism is required to achieve proper balance and the public need to start wising up to this 'franchising' of media, where journalists are restricted by strict company rules and are not free to report what they see or how they see it.

Principled people would refuse to work under those conditions. The left insist on a strong independent media, but what they mean is a united, controlled, politically correct, left-leaning media. Left and right wing representation needs to be present in all areas that significantly affect society. This way progressive attitudes are somewhat grounded by conservative knowledge. The development of AI (artificial intelligence), for example, would benefit from oversight from both left and right wing experts. If it is left under the sole control of people like the progressives who run Google, it won't take long for their politics and ideological outlook to become infused into every level of whatever is developed. A balanced left and right wing keeping an eye on things here would prevent this type of research and development from evolving into a cult that can be weaponised.

Even with parenting, it is common for mother and father to have slightly different views of how to handle the tantrums, etc. Unless they are the first two people in history to automatically agree on everything, this is effectively a left and a right wing. Both parents must be allowed to have input in order to try different things and work out what the family policy is going to be. If the soft side (not necessarily the female) always sets policy without fair discussion, maybe the children grow up to become brats.

The left and right are reference points within which debate can occur. Like left and right walls in a room, cancel out one reference point and the room collapses. No debate, no discussion, no space. At the moment the U.N. has less space inside it than a matchbox, no right wing at all. I would like to see one of two things occur: either completely defund it or create some space, by restructuring it with two independent wings with equal power and tight democratic controls... but preferably the former.

Divide Et Impera- Divide and Rule

This is the commonly known phrase used by Julius Caesar, also known as 'Divide and Conquer'. The principle is fairly well known: when faced with a large opponent, divide them into smaller groups, break their unity and then conquer them. What if someone were to take existing areas where some disagreement exists and boost them, giving them the spotlight via the media. Driving as many wedges as possible into the community to turn people against each other and stop the nation from being unified and speaking as one. The western media is as good at not reporting on some seemingly important events as it is at favouring ones that fit a certain agenda. So, how do they choose what is important and what is not?

Well, there is an interesting structure to the western mainstream media. Everyone knows about it and yet most people just sit there and accept it as the only way it can be. 95% of it is globally owned/ controlled by a small group of people. You can scan across channels and find the same news stories, the same headlines, the same message, even the exact same phrases on seemingly unrelated programs. This would not be possible with fully independent journalism. The media will take a movement and then shed light on it if it fits the agenda. What agenda? Why is it that Channel 9 never contradicts Channel 7 or the main newspapers? Certainly not on any serious subject.

Why have all mainstream media uniformly agreed that certain politicians are bad, and those that are sympathetic to the globalist agenda are to be respected? Regardless of why or how, it is the case that they speak as one organised entity. An entity that does not represent a democratically elected authority and does not follow a democratically agreed upon agenda. An entity that clearly takes orders from someone, on what to blacklist and which side to take in any issue. An entity which is not fairly representing society with a left and right wing.

Another Latin phrase comes to mind: *Cui bono? Who benefits?* When the mafia want to find out who is behind something, they are not bound by the same rules as detectives searching for admissible evidence. They will look at the common sense of the situation and the guilty party will often be standing in plain sight. Let us pretend we don't have to follow any rules or quote our sources and just look at the situation and see if there is an obvious source to this division. There are various social movements and political topics in existence in today's western world:

- Feminism
- Abortion
- Racism (or reverse racism, white privilege ideas, etc)
- LBGTXYZ,
- Gun control
- Climate change
- Donald Trump
- Immigration control/ refugee intake
- Border security
- Identity politics

These topics are all very polarising and for different reasons. Roughly 50% on each side of the various debates and it is not totally unreasonable to assume one's position on all of these based on one's opinion of one or two. That is to say, people tend to be mainly right wing or mainly left wing. But the mainstream media always sits on the left, often even creating a debate that barely exists. Why does the media always choose one side over the other? If the media switched to the right wing viewpoint, how many would switch with them? Would these issues even exist if the media stayed out of it or remained impartial and professional? Do they represent us or are they trying to steer us somewhere? If so, what are they trying to steer us towards and why are they all doing it so unanimously and effectively?

With Feminism and Racism they have unanimously decided that more women and non-white people need to be in charge and in powerful jobs and they want this to happen across all industries and regardless of the availability of suitably qualified people. They want diversity quotas and they want them now, they even have them now in many areas. They don't bother to help women and other races to become educated, connected, networking or otherwise qualified for these jobs, they just want the quotas met right now even if they aren't the best applicant.

Her body her choice. Pro-abortion is a part of the feminism movement. Again, why does the media take a side? There are legitimate arguments for not using tax payer funds to provide unlimited abortions to the public. It is one thing to make them 100% illegal, quite another to scrape out late term foetuses under Medicare. Late term abortions are hideous. If you are ok with abortion there is still no good reason for not deciding to do an abortion in the first trimester. Even then it is morally questionable and should only be a last resort for worst case scenario circumstances. Defenders of this will always throw the most unique, non-existent scenarios at you as an example of why abortions are necessary. "What about a 14 year old disabled girl with cancer, who was raped by her grandfather? Will she be forced to have her child even though it may kill her?"

Well, 99.99% of them are just women who chose not to use protection and don't want a kid right now, or possibly not with the guy they are with right now... or the football team they were with that weekend. Regardless of the motivation, there is a clear lack of morality somewhere along the line. The whole concept has become as normal as deciding what to have for dinner. Should we have a kid or not honey? Nah, I've got a lot on at work, let's get a doctor to slit its throat so nobody hears it scream and drag it out of you with meat hooks even though you've been growing it for 6 months and have just now changed your mind. It's ok, the government will pay for it.

With the LBGTXYZ movement we recently had a postal survey on gay marriage in Australia. This is an issue that wasn't even an issue. I don't even think I spoke to one person who objected to some sort of formal civil union being made between gay couples. They already had the right to adopt so that wasn't what was being debated. There were a few gaps in couple's legal rights, such as certain legal authority in hospital situations. Like visitation or power to flick the switch in extreme medical circumstances. So, instead of just patching the few gaps in the system, they had to march head first for full equality legally and socially, an amendment to the Constitution and strong support for anti-hate speech laws and education campaigns like Safe Schools. It is all we heard about for around three months, like there was nothing else going on in the world.

Sounds fair enough in theory, but even former Prime Minister John Howard pointed out that this was more complicated than it looked. The subtlest change in wording can have knock on effects that may not be initially realised. Almost every existing law is built on the Constitution, so one could argue that the wording of this Constitutional amendment should have been debated in some technical detail.

Take Christianity, for example. When you combine a few subtle changes to the Constitution with the new anti-hate speech laws you could potentially get a situation where preaching Christianity on television or in public becomes illegal. A seventy two year old Christian wedding cake shop owner refuses to celebrate a lesbian wedding with the same level of enthusiasm that she normally has for her work and we have a swat team jumping out of helicopters and kicking her doors in. Slight exaggeration, but I am yet to see any objection to a Muslim butcher refusing to sell bacon. The point is this:

In a Democracy there are things to discuss.

You can't just bluntly ram amendments to the Constitution into an unprepared public and expect no backlash. The postal vote was a vague overall indication of giving support or not supporting the right to gay marriage. They were confident the yes vote would win and the main reason so many people voted no was because they were either Christian or they just didn't trust the way it was being done, especially with government funds being used to take a side in the debate. Rainbow flags on buses, tax payer funded ads, bullying and harassment of church groups, etc. If it is a democracy, then surely the government's position shouldn't be decided upon until after the vote. Funding should not be provided by tax payers for an issue that tax payers are about to vote on. People who voted no were literally charged for the marketing that funded the Yes campaign. Why even bother asking us if the government is going to sponsor a massive campaign to favour one side of the debate?

The proposed amendments to the Constitution had not been shown to us, despite being written months or even years earlier. So, the more cautious and wise guardians of democracy showed concern before blindly following such otherwise honest and reputable politicians. Cough. On a more serious note; I wonder how the courts will decide how both partners can be awarded three quarters of everything when the first lesbian divorce occurs? That is what most women receive in divorce settlements isn't it? Just kidding... sort of.

Australia had massive name calling campaigns on social media. Any attempts to ask any technical questions were destroyed by the implication that suicides would immediately occur if the no vote won. I never knew good, honest Christians could be so open to attack from barefoot dreadlocked teenagers, unemployed buskers and other people who are otherwise never involved in politics. The fabric of democracy was torn apart for several months, all in the name of democracy. This proposal should have come from the left wing, not from the Liberal Party under a PM that no one ever even voted for. The lack of right wing representation and media coverage in the debate, if you can even call it a debate, made the right look like bigots, which we mostly aren't.

It was more like a sermon from the priests of our new universal religion. The vile behaviour of those promoting Yes actually caused many undecided people to vote No!! They actually drove many people to vote No!! In the end the Yes vote won, and I do support the principle of equality, so that is fine. Many right wingers voted yes; my point is that we should have been able to discuss it and work out how to address knock on issues, like religious protection, without causing total chaos in parliament for the next three years. I still don't know exactly what we voted for, I don't think anyone does. What actual legislative changes are going to follow? It was just a survey, the politicians do the voting on the actual laws.

The Safe Schools program is an example of the kind of hidden campaign that was intended to move forward in the slipstream of the marriage equality survey. The movement has been hijacked now by transsexualism and paedophilia. It's barely even about gay people anymore, they are now the boring old majority. Some of the gay people that I know don't even feel represented by the LBGT movement anymore. When did being gay become the same group as wanting to change gender? One thing is an action, a fact of who you are attracted to. The other is completely denying your biology and cutting off your penis, taking loads of hormones, often with fairly unconvincing results. If I were gay I would be annoyed that these two things are being put in the same minority category. I don't see what one has to do with the other.

Another example of the subtlety of such changes is whether it affects immigration law. Can Omar now marry his mate Mohammed to give him a green card and bypass immigration laws? Once here could they divorce and repeat, granting legal citizenship to an army of experienced militants all protected by the Constitution and before anyone with any authority notices? I'm sure someone would see what was going on and complain eventually but my question is, would it be legal? Would they be able to do it hundreds or thousands of times before the law was amended to close the gap?

We needed patriots at the level of George Washington drawing up and scrutinising these amendments from the left and right perspective, to properly debate the issues and ensure that there were no hidden gems. I do not trust most of our mainstream politicians to be so patriotically inclined. They barely pay attention as it is and usually just vote as they are told to by their leaders.

Case in point: Pauline Hanson formally asked the senate the question "Is it ok to be white?" The Liberal party members largely voted yes before realizing what was going on and clumsily changing their vote. The fact that they all voted yes without even looking into it first demonstrates that it isn't about the meaning of words any more. Rhetoric actually has some bearing, which is a dangerous concept. How will a sentence in a bill be viewed by future generations if the rhetoric of the era is different to the era of the creation of the bill?

Rather than the words alone having sufficient meaning, they are just following orders from whomever they have agreed to take their orders from, and they panicked when they thought they were signalling any right wing sentiment. I do not feel that the right wing was sufficiently represented by the Liberal party in 2018. Any Constitutional amendments should be debated by left and right wings and heavily tested before being implemented.

The Democrats in the USA are always pushing for National gun control. Their Constitution was specifically designed the way it was, because nobody trusted the Democrats with too much power. I really don't see how any of that has changed, other than to say that Republicans actually now trust Democrats less than they would have back then and based on recent behaviour quite rightly so. Again, we have the mainstream (left) media taking the very firm stance that guns should all be banned, or variations to that effect. It completely goes against the views of half of the community and yet they pick a side.

Whether you think I am right or wrong, my point is that the mainstream media are choosing sides and influencing the undecided people in the middle. They all but ignore legitimate objections regarding the existence of a well-armed militia and the right to defence against a suppressive government and pretend that gun control is the only rational choice. Their Second Amendment wasn't written to protect their right to hunt. The areas of highest gun violence are the ones with the strictest existing gun laws. Most school shootings occur in gun free zones. The Second Amendment was literally put in place to allow people to protect themselves to a greater or lesser degree from a tyrannical government. The type of government that the left are working overtime to put in place all around the western world.

This choice to pick a side was a conscious choice and it aligns with a larger agenda. They could easily take either side on this debate and put forward the facts accordingly, but instead of being unbiased they chose one side over the other proving that the dream that we have an unbiased media is up there with unicorns and fairies. In America the media actually created many of the anti-gun protests that occurred early 2018. The school kids all staged a walkout and almost every student in certain schools joined in, demonstrating that a day off school is always more attractive than actually learning about the Constitution.

The media set the date and place and all the kids had to do was follow the teachers. This was more than just taking a side, this was aggressively lead by the media under the guise of "angry students demand safety". Most of the kids don't even understand the significance of what is being protested. What kind of political movement is lead by kids anyway? Did they run out of adults who believed in the cause?

When Donald Trump announced that he wanted border security, the left all had a simultaneous stroke and started foaming at the mouth. They all thought about that one Mexican person that they met once at a party (even though he is probably not an illegal and is quite likely to be an Infowars subscriber and Republican, but they are so racist they can't tell the difference) and thanks to media exaggeration felt that Trump wanted to deport all Mexicans from the USA. When President Trump placed a temporary ban on travel from several nations identified by the CIA, during the Obama administration as being the highest risk of being a source of terrorism, the media labelled it Trump's Muslim ban. It didn't even affect 90% of the world's Muslim population. The media definitely took a side on this and to their own detriment.

Out of all the lefty viewpoints this is one of the easiest arguments to win. How could any nation call itself a nation without some form of functioning border and a desire to protect its citizens from a terrorist attack or diseases that only exist in the third world, in this day and age? Let them in! They all cried. The same country that experienced 9/11 was now crying "Open the borders, I'd rather be killed by a terrorist than be called a racist, free welfare for all". As if there would be no consequences at all. USA has already deported thousands of gang members since 2017. What do the left think these gang members do exactly? It's not humanitarian to put your own people at risk, that's just bad leadership.

It is treasonous and it's that kind of attitude that will ensure the Democrats do not have a U.S. president for the next 20 years. So, who benefits? Who benefits from causing this divide? Who would want the most powerful nations in the world to be weakened and divided by fighting amongst groups within themselves? Who is choosing the agenda and telling the media which side to be on in each instance? Is multiculturalism the chosen model because it is a series of smaller groups that can be easily manipulated into arguing with each other? Is someone trying to Divide and Rule?

If this division were present throughout all western countries then the globalist mainstream media would have full control over when and how to unleash a divide and conquer tactic, wouldn't they? Who would want to implement mechanisms that could allow the mainstream media to be capable of causing a division and lack of unity in western nations? Just having the capacity to load up our newspapers and 6pm dose of mainstream news with topics like "racism" and "gay marriage" is enough to cause arguments out in society and distract us from real international issues. This mechanism alone could be the building block on which the idea of multi culturalism was first strategically established. I can imagine someone saying: "We need a society that can be easily distracted by the media to keep our activity in the shadows".

Australia and the U.N.

Why do we have such a great country? Why are most other countries 2nd and 3rd world? After WW2 ended in 1945 the leading nations that won the war created the U.N. The terms 1st world country, etc were agreed upon at that time. It is not a statement of the wealth of the nation. These are the developed, capitalist, industrial countries aligned with the USA after WW2. The 2nd world countries are communist-socialist states, like China and Russia and the rest are 3rd world.

This alliance was earned by winning World War 2 against actual Nazis. The word Nazi is the abbreviation for the German translation of the National <u>Socialist</u> German Workers' Party. Remember that next time a mask-wearing ANTIFA member or a Green Peace supporting socialist calls someone a Nazi. Add to this 1st world status the fact that we are mineral rich, have a strong and technologically advanced navy and fairly good relations with most other countries and we are in a very strong position as a nation.

Essentially, the U.N. was a treaty established to stop the inevitable pattern of ongoing global domination through the game of empires expanding through warfare. Agreements and treaties were made amongst the first world countries and the world order was established. But, did it stop there or is the juggernaut slowly and quietly expanding? Over time the general public was left out of the loop as the various treaties and agreements were put in place. The model for a new global civilisation was being agreed upon by the various leaders and representatives and we are no longer required to have any input. You vote for this major party or that but they both follow the U.N. agenda regardless, so it is way out of our reach. The media report mainly on stories that push social buttons and draw support for the U.N. agenda or positively shape our view of the U.N.

The initial reason for founding the U.N. in 1945 was achieved and all was well. Economies were getting back on track and most of the world enjoyed a period of peace. The U.N. just sat there with no real purpose, or at least it seemed that way. Then it became about more than just preventing another global conflict, it started to see itself as a global government. Or at least some of the people within it saw that it could be used as a vehicle to create a world government.

Well, all of these U.N. representatives had to do something to justify their salaries. Along came the U.N.-backed campaigns that were pushed across all first world countries simultaneously. Democratisation of all nations was one of the early aims in the '50s. This opened the door to pushing dictators around in 2nd world countries and lead to Cuba being quarantined and cut off from trade with the USA. Various so-called "peace keeping" invasions continued throughout the following decades and the world has been in a different kind of war ever since, all in the name of democracy. It doesn't take much common sense to see that you can't force democracy onto people who aren't ready for it; democracy must be a grassroots movement supported by smaller groups with knowledgeable opinion leaders within the community. Not some "Astroturf" movement rolled on overnight by an external military force.

Many argued that U.N. peace keeping had become a tool for invading countries with oil and various other reasons like strategic locations. Kind of like the U.N. was leaning a little too much toward having an extreme capitalist philosophy for a period. Rightly or wrongly the national debt levels were good in 1st world countries reflecting that right wing leaning. Then it all changed some time in the early 80s and the US national debt began to skyrocket. Reagan enters office in 1981 and kick starts the economy out of recession, but the national debt continued to climb, and it has not gone down ever since.

So, where is all the extra expense and why can't anyone balance a budget anymore? U.N. contributions, on the face of it, have been around a billion dollars a year for the USA, so even after 50 years we are not talking 21 trillion dollars, which is their current national debt level. So how is the US debt getting up so high and so fast?

During Obama's two terms the national debt increased from $10.626 trillion to $19.947 trillion. The largest jump in any country's national debt level under anyone anywhere ever. When his first term started there was a period of recession, the GFC, which he had to get out of, but the way he did it is the kind of thinking that caused the GFC in the first place and may have set the world up for an even bigger crash, the next great depression.

There are several factors that go against the principles of sensible economics and tilt the above scale towards an increased national debt:

- Welfare and Healthcare entitlements.
- Foreign aid and U.N. contributions.
- War.
- Bad trade agreements.

These areas are the major reason the national debt keeps going up. Australia can be seen as a miniature version of the same model. There are differences but the overall basic reason for increased national debt is these primary points.

- The first one can be adjusted within a country by leaning towards socialism or capitalism.
- The second one seems to be decided by mainstream politicians and U.N. officials, regardless of who we vote for.
- The third one is mainly caused by chrony capitalists and Neocons in powerful positions.
- The last is being run through the U.N. as a means of lowering the economy of 1st world countries.

The social reform campaigns that are being pushed through the U.N. appear to be aimed at ultimately creating global socialism with obedient citizens, who think what they are told to think. Look at the basic concept of a democracy and now tell me which U.N. official you voted for or which U.N. treaty we discussed and debated as a democratic nation, before signing up for huge tax expenditure. I was never consulted on any of this and the strategy the U.N. employs to address their problems was never debated as a public issue.

Does the U.N have a two-party-preferred structure to allow for debate from all angles of society and includes the ebbs and flows in normal social evolution? Are any controls in place to prevent the U.N from being completely hijacked by influential world trillionaires who have monopolies over industries and unlimited corporate controls in place? The same can be said of the E.U. (European Union) - not one democratically elected official. The whole concept is a total bypass of democracy and the democratic process of voting. Democracy is being able to remove rules and add them as society debates the issues and moves with the times.

The U.N. is supposed to be nothing more than an alliance, formed after WW2. Does an alliance usually have its own Constitution like an independent nation? The U.N. charter seems innocent and virtuous enough but it is laced with agreements and goals that can be very difficult to achieve and can be selectively prioritised alongside another hidden agenda.

Don't try to tell me that Malcom Turnbull (who Australia didn't even vote for anyway) sat there and contributed to the U.N. agenda. It is not put together by our elected world leaders sitting around a big table and representing their nation. The overall strategy and format is set by some unseen group, the elected officials sit in their seats and are told where to sign. Well, at least that was the routine until President Trump came along and started saying "No".

The U.N. was established as an alliance of nations to prevent WW3 and at some stage it became an independent organism and developed its own higher purpose. A progressive entity with social reform at the top of its agenda, restructuring the entire planet. If it is progressive in nature that automatically makes it anti-conservative, maybe this explains where the anti-conservative movement is coming from. The lefties are attacking Christianity on all sides and they are on steroids. They have been injected with confidence because the U.N. has a similar leftist ideology and has united them across the planet. The U.N. representatives and leaders, the mainstream media, Hollywood, the education system, the police system and even the legal system are pushing these social reform campaigns through the left side of politics, but they all get a power boost from the U.N.

It's really no different to anything involving human nature. For example when a bikie gang gets 'patched over' it becomes more powerful as a result of their interstate connections. Their confidence comes from more powerful people and interstate connections creating space for them. This is why Donald Trump has had such an impact on western countries. He is the first person to say "No" to them in a long time and he just keeps on going, putting his own people first. I wish someone would put Australia first for a change. We could be a global powerhouse in world energy with our vast land, natural perimeter and mining resources. You might say it is girt by sea and abounds in nature's gifts of beauty rich and rare.

Without digging too deeply you can generally tell when something is a U.N. backed campaign because it instantly appears in all first world countries and is instantly agreed upon by all government officials, universities, Hollywood celebrities, opinion leaders and general left-leaning groups. These campaigns appear to have organic roots but if that were actually true, they would not appear so uniformly and overwhelmingly across all of the first world nations.

You can read the U.N. agenda on the website <u>un.org</u>. It has evolved from its original charter into something very suspicious. The charter can be purchased online for $1. The socialistic material that is becoming so prominent in western society originates directly from U.N. resolutions. They are very open about it. The U.N. charter has certain goals and I agree with at least most of them, on face value. What I am opposed to is how they are attempting to solve problems with socialistic thinking and how these "virtuous" goals are being used to manipulate our world leaders into bypassing democracy and destabilising our society and economy at home.

If the following circumstances were to be implemented what would the world look like?

- **An undemocratic one world government.** National governments being forced to follow international treaties which effectively bypass the capacity to vote against them.
- **A new universal ideology.** The natural product of multiculturalism. Assuming it doesn't descend into civil war, the group will eventually find some fundamental overriding ideology that they can all agree on.
- **Restrictions on freedom of speech.** Anti-hate speech laws being increased and enforced more and more.
- **A socialistic/welfare driven structure.** Western countries are already being asked to sign harsh trade restrictions and to commit to enormous foreign aid contributions, which are effectively welfare on a world scale. Socialism ends up bankrupt every time, so what does that mean for the world economy if it has a socialistic structure?
- **Massively powerful technology giants.** The ability to instantly delete or silence opposing opinion leaders, delete their income streams, prevent their messages from spreading. The ability to spy on people and label them based on their political or religious views. Social credit score penalties for people falling outside of the new world leaders' preferred attitudes. A system they already use in China.
- **Artificial Intelligence.** The tech giants automate their processes and allow the matrixes to think for them, choosing automatically which Facebook pages to delete, for example. Is it possible that this could occur? Isn't it already being done to some degree by an automatic matrix?

I draw attention to the following excerpts from the 2015 U.N General Assembly:

General Assembly
Seventieth Session

Sustainable Development Goals
Goal 1: End poverty in all its forms everywhere.
Goal 2: End hunger, achieve food security and improved nutrition and promote sustainable agriculture.
Goal 5: Achieve gender equality and empower all women and girls.
Goal 10: Reduce inequality within and among countries.

- *10.3 Ensure equal opportunity and reduce inequalities of outcome, including by eliminating discriminatory laws, policies and practices and promoting appropriate legislation, policies and action in this regard.*
- *10.5 improve the regulation and monitoring of global financial markets and institutions and strengthen the implementation of such regulations.*

So, rather than existing to prevent the next major world war, the U.N. is now concerned with gender equality and regulating the economy to reduce inequality of outcome? Quite a jump in scope and what does it really mean to regulate something? The risks to our economy and democracy here are staggering and yet the average person is plodding along completely unaware that we are heading directly towards this type of global socialist structure, because they don't want people to accuse them of saying "I don't care about ending world hunger".

Agenda 21 is a book released by the U.N. It is not easy to read but many compelling interpretations of it have been written by conspiracy theorists. The use of key statements in the charter have evolved into an aim to equalize everyone under a new central government. The best argument in defence of this one world government structure that anyone can come up with is:

"But, but, but that would never happen" or "The modern world is civilised now, I'm sure they would put safeguards in to prevent bad people from taking over." Well, what safeguards?

Come on people! Don't trust them so easily! Look at everything these people have done for us so far: Wars, suppression of technology, censoring free speech, big pharma profiting from doping up our kids, Mainstream media lying endlessly. No, I'm sure all the "grown-ups" in charge of this new, unregulated global powerhouse are going to be very honest about how the most centralised global power hierarchy that ever existed is going to be used. What could possibly go wrong with so much power being put in one place? Imagine lodging a complaint with the U.N. because your farming town has gone bankrupt due to their trade restrictions. It is hard enough being heard in our current system and that is democratic and locally run!

Wanting to end hunger and poverty is a legitimate goal and one that we all share, but not at all costs and not putting everyone at risk of financial collapse in the process. So, how exactly do they plan to do it? Are they going to do it by increasing my taxes and just giving it away like a global welfare program making me the modern-day slave, leading to my country falling into another great economic depression like the 1920s? That is what it looks like. The Paris Trade Agreement includes restrictions on how many cows we can produce in 1st world countries. Even if cow emissions were an environmental issue, you'd think you would have to restrict them in all countries to be effective, wouldn't you?

Under this new "fair" world structure how many hours per week would I have to work to achieve a similar lifestyle to what I have today? Would it even be possible? Welfare has held minority communities back more than it has helped them in the western world. An entire welfare class has emerged in the U.K. so why should it work any better on a larger scale?

The African population is the fastest growing in the world. How will that play out in the long term with the poorest education standards in the world and an ever-increasing dependence on foreign aid? What if my nation enters a recession or economic depression? Do they still take our tax money away then, even though I am now struggling to keep a roof over my head? What does my life look like when it is adjusted down to the wealth level of the average citizen of Earth? When all countries achieve this equal utopian, nirvana state; "Equality of outcome". I'd say that adjusted lifestyle would resemble something that can be currently found in a 2nd or 3rd world country, at best. Where will the virtue signalling Hollywood celebrities be when this happens? Still in their Hollywood mansions, of course. They are all hundreds of millions of dollars ahead of you and I.

Goal 5: Achieve gender equality and empower all women and girls. Well, it's not really that far away from 2030 right now and I don't see any 'empowering' going on in Saudi Arabia or any 3rd world countries. Do you? I haven't seen one campaign aimed at areas of the globe where actual gender inequality exists.

All I see is virtue signalling and complaining from Hollywood celebrities that women in western countries are paid less on average than men, or are insufficiently represented in politics. In the first world women actually have more legal rights than men, look at divorce laws and how things are worked out to favour one gender over another. Men still paying crippling alimony even after both partners remarry, even if the new husband is rich!

Then we move down to 10.3 and they actually use the term 'inequalities of outcome'. I am all for equal opportunity and offering education to people in poor areas. But inequality of outcome?! This means taxing the winners permanently to prop up the losers. It is literally what Marxism is all about, which is proven to lower initiative and drive and ultimately leads to rich people opting out of risky ventures and crashes the economy.

The supposed 'good intentions' of the U.N. have been completely taken over by the sort of thing you expect from the far left of the left wing of any western nation. People who are pushing for global socialism/communism. The various mouth pieces and representatives of the U.N. may think they are doing the right thing because they themselves are lefties. They see lots of images of hungry African kids and we are reminded daily about climate change, so we decide not to object to anything U.N., but we have never had any reasonable democratic discussion on how these issues should be addressed and before the Paris Agreement there were never really any firm agreements that affected our sovereignty to this degree.

This could be the end of democracy, free speech, free market capitalism and the end of human nature as we know it.

This push to create global equality of outcome is pure communism.

I don't have a problem with the intention to solve world hunger. I do have a problem with them using that as a reason to completely bypass and overthrow national sovereignty and democracy while implementing economic controls and promoting a socialist welfare structure that I don't believe will be sustainable. Where are the U.N. resolutions to liberate suppressed technology that could benefit society? Where is the global enforcement and expansion of the Geneva convention? Why hasn't the U.N. issued any effective action plan to rescue thousands of practitioners of Falun Gong being permanently imprisoned by the bus load in China. Why are they trying to ban the use of coal, when that is actually the cleanest fuel we have, other than nuclear? The first version of an electric car was invented in 1832, where are all the electric cars if the combustion engine is the cause of the pollution? Surely the U.N. could have come up with something better than trade restrictions on cows to address these issues?

If they believe their own vast exaggerations of the climate change 'science', why hasn't the U.N. been furiously pressuring the oil companies to sell or use the patents to the electric car, or convincing the American government and people to pass a law, making it illegal to suppress supposedly 'planet saving' technology? Why do they use pictures of wind farms in their promotional material, when the overall carbon footprint of these plants is higher than the total footprint per KW of the old style of coal power plant?

Electric cars combined with plenty of nuclear power plants or highly efficient emissions recycling coal power plants would be a major step forward in CO2 emissions reduction. Sadly, I came up with that solution myself, as nothing like that has ever been a public issue or a genuine U.N. topic.

Maybe they planned to tackle that kind of thing after they implement economic controls and usurp total world domination? The truth is that if climate change were the real issue there would be many other ways to address it, but instead they started charging 15c for plastic bags at Coles and using Climate change action as a carrot to bait us into implementing a one world government. Then, once they have the economic controls in place the real game begins. That is when the full agenda for a new world order would have begun to roll out.

We never voted on any of these issues, we never elected any of the officials or representatives that designed the overall strategies. We never had any chance to give feedback on any of it and yet we are giving away our sovereignty inch-by-inch to the U.N. because they talk about starvation and gender inequality from their expensive black tie, taxpayer-funded and first class catered, international events. They are deciding the fate of the entire world, while being serviced like Lords and Earls of Downton Abbey and being flown in on private jets. How did so much authority fall into the hands of such a small group of unelected, career driven people? When were these people chosen to represent us and how? I don't remember voting for any of the U.N. representatives.

Foreign aid in regular payments doesn't solve anything long term. A famine requires urgent but temporary aid and assistance. General poverty is not a shortage of food, as there is plenty of food in the world. It is a shortage of production and therefore a short-fall of exchange with the people producing the food. This global welfare model creates an environment that can allow them to sell us the idea of a "responsible" one world government that supposedly 'ends poverty in all forms everywhere' by reducing the amount of trade we can do. Wouldn't this just put Australians out of work? How do we end poverty by closing factories and shrinking agriculture, creating poverty?

The way out of African nations' permanent bad economy is the same thing that got western nations out of our last great depression. Democratic capitalism, a two-party-preferred system with sovereignty and free speech. Not welfare, diversity quotas, market trade controls and an elitist group of rich aristocrats in ivory towers. The current U.N. strategy is exactly what you would come up with if you were following the step-by-step principles of The Communist Manifesto, by Karl Marx. Needless to say, that is exactly what they are doing.

The economic systems are not designed to build on successful actions of past successful groups, they are designed to overthrow self-governance of all nations simultaneously, under one central government and with a socialist economic structure. The wealthiest nations permanently subsidising the poorest nations to 'eradicate poverty'. If trade is controlled, each nation becomes little more than a retailer of specific products in a department store, where the rent and trading conditions are set by the store management, the U.N.

The system is designed to manage the decline of the world economy in the name of climate change and equality. The economists and bankers know that socialism doesn't work. They have all agreed that the world is running out of resources. They have engineered a cunning, soft plan that people will not only go along with but the more naïve of us will insist upon. Manipulating the left is how socialism is brought in anywhere it has been tried and it has always failed.

Consider how many people are willing to accept democratic socialism now in their own nation. This is the tipping point. We need public informed discussion on what socialism is to get us away from this tipping point. Only then will people really start to question the strategies of the U.N. in an informed manner. Until there is a decent understanding of exactly what socialism is, we will be surrounded by too many unthinking sheep to stop it. The intentions of the U.N. charter are fine, in principle but the structure and strategy being put forward puts too much power in one place and goes against the very reason the U.N. was founded in the first place. They want to take over the world to stop someone like Hitler taking over the world.

Our nation will continue to walk toward this unless we all start waking up and engaging in politics right now, the only way this can be done is with an independent right wing media. Ideally this should receive the same funding that the ABC receives now. This is one way to restore the balance that is missing in the U.N. The U.N. is not a libertarian or conservative group. It is not built on Christian or democratic principles. The theme of the charter is all about equality which, like all religions, can be interpreted in extreme fashion by zealots. It is disconnected from direct input by all citizens of all nations. Only selected people can join this group. Who does the hiring? It does not have a left and right two-party-preferred structure with term limits and national votes with public debate over strategies and priorities.

What if it were to become dominated by career driven people with more left-leaning sentiment, much like the mainstream media? Socialist leaning sentiment? What if measures were in place to stop right wingers being members or from becoming too influential? Even if their intentions were true and their plan was based on flawless climate science, the potential for just one error puts the entire human race at great risk. One mistake and the world economy crashes and we run out of food. Too much left thinking leads to socialistic solutions. This model fails 100% of the time, if human history is any indication. Centralised power at that level is just too risky and with no real democratic controls in place it is a ticking time bomb that is being too heavily contributed to by people on the far-left side of politics.

If climate change science were discussed openly and on an equal playing field, most of the deception and selective use of data would be brought out and the whole argument would fall into a heap on the ground. Have you noticed that they called it global warming until the globe started to cool again? Now it is called climate change. That is why they do not want that type of informed public debate to occur. Scientists with contradictory evidence, such as hard evidence that variation in sunspots have contributed significantly to fluctuations in Earth's temperature, are labelled Climate Change Deniers and harassed, etc.

It is similar to how archaeologists or geologists providing hard evidence that the pyramids are older than 6000 years have been treated, as can be seen in the documentary 'The Pyramid Code'. Geology is a separate science to archaeology. If they are both right, then on analysis of the data available they should both produce exactly the same timeline but they don't. Geology is the more scientific science in the scenario addressed in that documentary, but there is an overriding sub-culture that is heavily controlled, so the senior science is thrown out the window. Controlled by whom?

This is the type of thing that the founders of the United States of America were addressing when they implemented the electoral college. That is the system the Democrats are complaining about right now and have been trying to change since it was first established. They did not trust the elites to represent all citizens fairly and so votes were distributed strategically to stop the richest cities, like New York and Washington from having too much control over their much denser populations. The problems that the founding fathers of America identified and handled very effectively in their Constitution are the very same flaws that are present in the U.N. and potentially any group of people.

Plastic in the ocean and deforestation are separate issues to global warming. They are also serious environmental issues that can be addressed with good management and that is exactly what is starting to happen. It is also worth noting that 90% of the plastic in the ocean comes from just ten rivers, two in Africa and eight in Asia. So, to address this California bans straws and Coles charges us 15c now for plastic bags.

Climate change is something different. It is an endless pit of unknowable mystery that causes anxiety and panic on a global scale (well, unless you're the banks, who still seem happy to lend thirty year mortgages to people for ocean front property developments). The media reminds us that the oceans are about to rise daily, even though they never do. They seem to think it will be solved by moving all of the factories over the China, limiting the number of cows we can have and the rest of the plan hasn't been fully explained to us yet... I'm sure it has nothing to do with the U.N. using its newfound economic controls and our ever-increasing national debts to shrink and control our economy more and more.

In the name of climate control they could impose some harsh emission restrictions such as our right to build our own factories or the right to have farms with cows. I refer specifically to the controls that were briefly mentioned in 10.5 of the 2015 Sustainable Development Goals and built in to the U.N. Paris agreement. See, they touch on it in the General Assembly, which is made publicly available on their website and then go in to the more gruesome details in the small print in treaties and international agreements that only experts can understand.

Even if you disagree and feel that my concerns are 100% wrong, it is still possible that this type of decision can be made behind closed doors. There is still the undisputed fact that democracy is being bypassed. There is nothing you can do about it if we allow any central world government to be built any further. I do not feel represented in the U.N., do you? I feel that the U.N. appears to be making some very left-leaning and one world government leaning decisions. This is the problem. If it looks like a duck and it quacks, then it's a duck. To me, the U.N. looks like a small group of lefties trying to take control of the world.

Beyond Blue

Another item mentioned in these U.N. resolutions is the availability of Universal healthcare and mental health services. Jeff Kennett was paid to found Beyond Blue in the year 2000 to raise awareness of Depression and prostate cancer. An unlikely pairing of causes but I remember when it was founded and the types of discussions that were happening around town. When somebody objected to the system of treating depression with drugs the well-groomed hipster fund raisers could just say, "yeah but it's about prostate cancer and general men's health and stuff man."

Geoff Gallop was suddenly and very publicly struck down with this affliction now being defined as an "illness" and he pushed the line "I am sick and going to see my doctor." This was the first time we were exposed to the idea that depression or any mental health issue was an illness that could be treated by a doctor. The mainstream media were hanging off his every word. Before then I had never seen a depressed person receive so much attention and praise. Fifteen years later and the campaign has expanded to include anxiety and generally raise awareness for anti-discrimination. In the Beyondblue Strategic Plan 2015-2020 The Hon. Jeff Kennett can be quoted as saying:

> *"We don't just focus on raising awareness anymore, we work to influence behaviour change: at both individual and system levels."*

So, just like the U.N. the scope of the campaign has expanded and now it has become their business to change our behaviour both individually and <u>at a systemic level</u> if we are contributing to suicide, depression or anxiety. Well, what exactly does that mean? Are they helping anxious people adapt to the real world, or are they expecting everyone else to change to tip toe around, so as not to trigger them? Safe spaces everywhere, for everyone.

This has become the norm in almost every aspect of government, and this radical left-leaning attitude has now reached the pinnacle of political correctness gone mad in the US. The general attitude of the Social Justice Warriors (SJW) has very firmly become:

'Do exactly what we say or else.
Also, we will change the rules frequently.'

Like a highly organised ant colony, their queen decides on a target and they attack it. Top of their list at the moment: White conservative men. Attack anyone doing well and distribute the spoils to the people at the bottom.

The problem with this philosophy is that it has the same basic principles as the economic principles of socialism but on a social level. Reward the losers and punish the winners. It turns society on its head and what has it produced? "The Millennial". The guy who can't start a lawnmower but knows that we need definitely gun control. The guy who worships the authority of law only when it suits his argument. The expert on everything as long as he can have three minutes to google it and make sure he knows what his peers think first. The gender confused, gender lacking and multi-gendered and sadly the nine-year old transsexuals. The leftist philosophy is flawed.

What was built to help suicidal people, using tax payer and donated money has now become the oppressor of free speech seeking to make changes to our society and culture at a systemic level. Across these globalist platforms it has been decided that toxic masculinity has got to go and handbag wearing, limp wristed beta males are the new "in thing". Why? To supposedly reduce suicides? Even though suicide rates increase with every move they make.

So, since reducing suicides is the main reason for this charity existing what has it done for suicide stats? Well, under the influence of similar programs suicide rates have <u>increased</u> in the USA over the past ten years by around 20% since 2007 to around 45,000 per year. In Australia the rates are around 2,866 per year, not nearly as high as USA but still up around 10% from 2007 and still quite high given the population size. This is age standardised stats and averages taken per 100,000 people to remove population fluctuation from the data. So, what is this program actually achieving? Is it promoting a theoretical solution that isn't working?

Yes… Yes, it is.

They will argue that it will only work if they have more rules and more change and that it wasn't fully implemented last time but that's what they always say. Clearly the underlying philosophy is flawed. If it worked it would give an instant and significant result, especially given the size and scope of the movement and funding.

It is another example of the wrong ideological attitude and it is not by accident. These Trojan horse campaigns are all being run through the U.N. The ideology that is validated by the mainstream viewpoint is psychology/ psychiatry and those sciences have been built on a socialistic approach to addressing problems. Don't confront the real problem, invent a new and even bigger problem instead.

The type of therapy the corporate pharmaceutical world is thriving on is the kind that helps people to "tolerate" their existing environment. They give you drugs to ease the pain, instead of helping you become proactive in dealing with your problems and outwardly create the environment you desire. This is an essential ingredient to the social reform agenda.

Mass social reform on a global scale would not want people to be well mentally equipped to oppose it, it would want people to tolerate it as it grows. This shift towards chemical therapy in lieu of counselling slots neatly in with a design to pave the way for the bigger movement. A progressive movement of "tolerance" and plenty of money being made in the process, of course.

In other times the religious groups would be the ones you turned to for spiritual help, i.e. depression, anxiety loss of direction, etc. Nowadays, the doctors are our first port of call and this is what is being pushed in the mainstream. The general structure of these movements is that they appear to help, they are structured so that opposing them makes you look like the bad guy. But ultimately these programs don't work, they don't produce the product that is the intended purpose of the program. The more they fail the more they gear up to expand, citing that they require more funding or more power to properly implement their plans and achieve their goals.

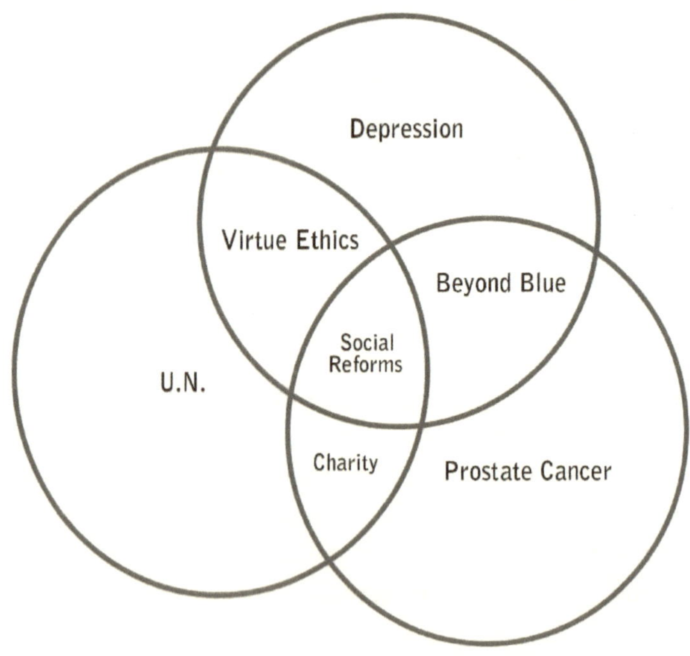

The Venn diagram above demonstrates that certain areas have significant common ground. The senior goal of social reform is shared by the U.N. and Beyond Blue. This creates a cohesive environment where they work together to achieve the common goals. All U.N. initiatives align to other causes as much as possible. This strategy allows the U.N. to quickly gain allies and in this instance "sell" the idea of social reform to large audiences. If you had to sell social/cultural reform to a group of people what would you do? It's not an easy thing to do: Sell the idea of 'completely changing your culture' to a group that otherwise is doing well.

How would you "sell" methane emission controls to a country? You might find an area where some of your existing supporters are already trying to discourage a certain industry from existing and find some common ground.

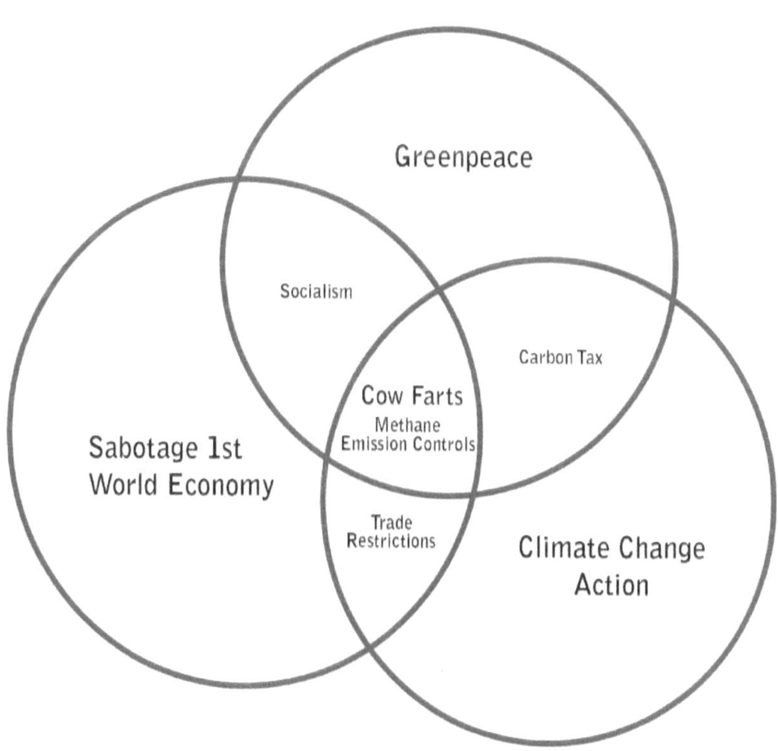

Greenpeace supporters are already largely vegan or vegetarian and they are mostly socialists nowadays anyway. Selling the idea of reducing cow farming is an easy sell. They tried sabotaging our economy with a carbon tax. They are still pushing for outright banning coal, which would destroy Australia's economy. Now emission controls through reduced cow production has a common ally in vegetarians. Is this 'methane emissions cause climate change' theory based on robust climate change science or is it just the path of least resistance in a tense political climate with a bonus aspect of harming the national economy?

Universal Belief System

Psychology/Psychiatry fits with the definition of at least a major part of a universal ideology that can operate over existing religions. We have doctors and psychiatrists that are Muslim, Christian and Atheist for example. It is not uncommon these days for members of any religion to seek help from a doctor for depression or anxiety. Actual therapy these days is only a small part of the treatment that is offered for people requiring help with mental health issues. The main approach to treating issues is to take drugs, nulling the pain.

The theory may be that the person is calmer when on the drugs and therefore more able to think clearly to resolve their issues but how does that explain people being stuck on drugs for ten or twenty years? The approach to treatment is very corporate, and it seems more interested in calming a person down to make them quieter in the short term, for everyone else's benefit, rather than helping the person to resolve their underlying problems. This is the ideology that is being defaulted to as being the modern-day version of what used to be the role of religion. It is very compatible with the new age leftist ideology. Rather than empowering the person asking for help, they are squashing them further down toward silence and conformance by doping them up. If you think about it, psychology is actually structured very much like a religion.

The original definition of psychology is 'the study of the human soul'. It is derived from the Latin words:

'Psyche' the human soul or spirit; and
'ology" the study of something.

Dictionary.com gives us this definition for Religion:
Noun.

1) *A set of beliefs concerning the cause, nature and purpose of the universe, especially when considered as the creation of a superhuman agency or agencies, usually involving devotional and ritual observances, and often containing a moral code governing the conduct of human affairs.*

There are certain things that all religions have in common:

- They denounce or suppress the authority of other religions/philosophies as far as treatment for mental health issues is concerned and claim to have all the answers.
- They make statements that cannot be scientifically verified making them hard to challenge. (for example; in psychiatry ADHD is caused by chemical imbalances in the brain, yet no solid reference to what the correct balance is or any genuine method to scientifically test for it).
- Statements are made with supreme authority. Much like a religious zealot, there is no room for discussion or debate in psychiatry unless you are qualified and very senior in their ranks. Discussions were had by the professionals, so you don't need to worry about doing that now. Just pop this pill (no need to read the suicide warning on the side of the bottle either, I'm sure people hardly ever commit suicide when they are on these opioids...)

Like a witch hunt in medieval times or the Spanish inquisition, think about how the hate speech laws are now being enforced more than ever against conservative voices. If the U.N. programs are progressive, social reform campaigns that must mean conservative views are in direct conflict with their goals. No wonder they enforce hate speech laws so disproportionately. This is a new religion erasing the old one.

As well as checking-in to our devices several times a day to pray to our universal Big Brother technology corporation, another similar concept that would contribute to a universal belief system can be seen in the subject of climate change. You can literally show people that sea levels haven't risen since Al Gore's 'An Inconvenient Truth' was released in 2006 and they will still not hear it.

You can always find government funded official projections of what 'would' happen 'if' sea levels rose, but no mention of the fact that the sea has not risen at all. So, where is the actual water? The city of Perth is cut in half by the Swan River. This average position of the river bank has not changed at all in my lifetime. The Sydney Opera house is still there, photos from the early 1900s show the water at the same level. You don't have to look hard to find all kinds of complex, difficult to read projections and warnings about how our cities will be under water in 10 years (I was reading these reports 15 years ago).

Water finds its level, that is how the bubble in a spirit level works. If it rises in one part of the world due to melting polar ice caps then logic dictates that on average it will rise everywhere evenly, with the only variance being that the Earth's tectonic plates can twist as they move. This explains the occasional loss of an island, usually along the edge of the tectonic plate region. This commonsense logic is something that you can just observe yourself. No need to email anyone a link to an article that was written by a person who is paid by Rupert Murdoch. You can just look outside and see if the river is the same as it was when you were a child. Man-made climate change is what binds them and blinds them. The need to address it urgently and at all costs is the belief system that binds the Greenpeace activists together and blinds them to the logic of basic economics and sovereignty and the dangers of a borderless society or a one world government.

Respect for the environment is extremely important and nowhere on Earth demonstrates that more than western capitalist nations. We do this by constantly improving technology, such as the latest coal power plants, which recycle their own emissions for a second burn, for example. Generation 4 nuclear power plants are physically impossible to put into meltdown without violating the laws of physics. Many other options have been discovered and made viable, such as liquefying the CO2 and pumping it 1km beneath the ocean where the CO2 is absorbed and will remain permanently after forming crystal hydrate with the sea water. So, instead of looking at these, the U.N. wants to ban the use of coal outright. Maybe that is because it aligns more with the equality of outcome portion of the charter, controlling the economy and holding 1st world countries back allowing the other nations to catch up (in theory).

The Banks have the most to lose here and plenty of resources to do their own research. However, they don't seem to believe the hype either because they are still willing to lend billions of dollars in mortgages on river front property over thirty year loans without any form of federal climate change insurance policy in place. The hardcore socialists simply don't care because they think the world is going to flood if we don't halt capitalism immediately and their only source of media is the ABC and SBS. They are the zealots of a new age religion, the modern day version of Hitler's brown shirts and with modern psychology, the basic ingredients of a universal religion that will expand by force is in the making. Climate change has everyone feeling anxious, Big Pharma has the drugs for that, universal healthcare will even pay for it, costing the nation billions and driving us further into debt. That leads us to the final piece of the new religion.

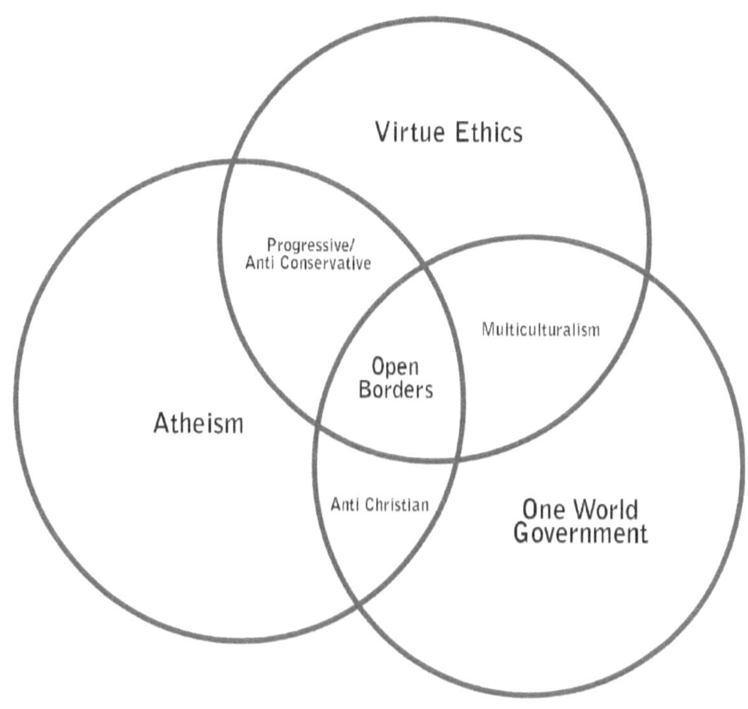

Attacking Christianity is a common theme with the above three movements. Open borders and multiculturalism is a key component in watering down Christian influence over western nations. I don't see Saudi Arabia, China, Turkey or any other countries being asked by the U.N. to open their borders to increase diversity or to promote multiculturalism. Only in western countries, founded on Christianity. If multiculturalism is such a great thing, wouldn't they want everyone to have it? Shouldn't 3rd world immigrants be happy to upgrade to 2nd world countries as well? It is still an upgrade and it would allow them to be safe from whatever they were supposedly escaping, or is the express lane to our 1st world country the only reasonable choice? I use the term "multicultural" here, not "multiracial". There is nothing wrong with a nation having people from all backgrounds and races as productive members of the group.

I don't see any problem with countries having their own sovereignty and building on trade relations to implement any necessary restrictions on things like pollution, extinction of species and harm to the ocean. This system keeps everyone in the present with power being available to withdraw from discussions if it seems like someone is not playing fair. The danger of a central global system is that there is no power to withdraw.

Even if you elect someone like Donald Trump it would still take decades to untangle and withdraw from some of the complex treaties that the U.N. has set up and is trying to further push to tie us into the central, world government system. Just one mistake and the whole system could be taken over by people capable of applying pressure in the right way.

To use their own language there is safety in 'diversity' and that means diversity of nations and diversity in the balance of power. Diversity across the planet of different government systems, different ideologies. Different ways to survive as groups. If one system fails or hits a rough patch, the others could offer advice or short-term aid to help them and learn from where they went wrong, such as learning about every time throughout history socialism has been tried. If we become one big group under one hierarchy and it fails, there is no safety net. All our eggs in one giant basket.

The Architects

The architects behind this are geniuses. I have to hand it to them. I mean they are pure evil. But they are very smart. The foresight and influence that they must have had back when these programs were put in motion is inconceivable. They have managed to fund the whole operation using mainly taxpayer money and make enormous profits along the way. They gradually chipped away at society with their media outlets to create controllable angry mobs. The confidence they've had in their capacity to constantly push the media along the lines and constantly shape public opinion is incredible. The clever tactic of always appearing to do good at each stage whilst building up to a point where the public can be sold on socialism or a one world government, an idea that would have had you chased down the street by any member of society just fifty years ago. To be honest, I'm not sure if the original U.N. charter was designed to be abused or if they have just seen a weakness and slowly built a strategy around it.

Conspiracy theorists will tell us that the people that funded the Nazis are the same people which were influential in drafting the U.N. charter leading up to 1945. Whether this is true or not seems to me to be irrelevant. The fact is that the U.N. should not even have a charter. It is a basic alliance, an agreement that the most powerful nations will talk to each other first and try to work things out before entering full blown war. There is no need to take the alliance any further than that. There will always be people trying to increase their power and influence over their area, whether it is a chief of police, a judge or the CEO of a super market chain.

This is why the structure of any government is so important. Our system has been shaped and tested over hundreds of years of democratic existence, economic fluctuations and wars in various western nations. It should not be thrown out now and replaced with something which appears to be structured as communism just because someone said "climate change" or because someone said "tranny" on YouTube and that is offensive (apparently).

George Bush Senior referred to the New World Order on several occasions, Obama has referred to the New World Order in several speeches during his presidency. Towards the end of 2015 he also mentioned a coming recession that the world would have to brace for, a recession that his masters engineered. Yet, at the time of this writing this has not actually happened. It was reversed by President Trump by simply pulling out of most of the trade deals Obama made and allowing the economy to thrive organically, with less restrictions. In 1991 David Rockefeller thanked the media for not shedding light on their plans for the world. Visit YouTube and search:

"David Rockefeller speech will give you the chills".

In this speech he literally admits to breaking the law to put certain things in place with the intention of world domination. Just admitting planning to do that is treason. If Hillary had won 2016, the final pieces of the New World Order would have been put in place and we would now be hearing the media celebrating a restructure of global power. A common sense approach to restructuring society to address irreversible national debt levels would be being discussed right now. Protecting our planet from climate change and protecting minorities from hate speech and social injustice by implementing democratic socialism across all 1st world countries would be being celebrated and welcomed by the mainstream media.

It is time to put the power back in the systems that were built to service democracy. Democratic two-party nations. This blurring of the lines between sovereign nations and the U.N. is exposing all of us to major economic dangers and the risk of being hijacked by a one world government. It is our responsibility to discuss these issues and be willing to hear opinions that you may not agree with. Ironically the architects are the ultimate capitalists and are the reason people have a problem with capitalism in the first place. They are the ones sponsoring the anti-capitalism movement. Well, why would they be the ones who want to give up their billionaire lifestyles? Maybe it's the belief that they are trading that for something even better?

The platform for the Democrats in America in late 2018 is implementing democratic socialism, opening the borders and completely restructuring the world under a central government. They even road tested the idea of removing the job of the president and changing the structure so that there isn't one. That's code for communism. They have used the worst aspects of extreme capitalism to bully and censor alternative media sources and basically stifle people from objecting to their plans for world domination.

You might think you are playing chess and you can debate with these people. But chess is in 2D and they are playing 3D chess, they own the board too. If you start to look like you're winning they shake the board and keep shaking it until it tips in their favour again. These guys are everything that they accuse others of and worse. Only our firm commitment to democracy and freedom of speech can defend us against them, that has always been our best defence. Fortunately, President Trump has been playing 4D chess and cut them off at the knees, just in the nick of time.

Today they ban Infowars, tomorrow they delete your Facebook account because you liked a post by Cory Bernadi. Communist China has implemented full blown social control through their social media platforms, directly penalising people with outspoken opinions or alternative views. Even awarding social penalities for buying alcohol.

China is a full-blown communist society, but the digital algorithms used by Google could easily be duplicated in our western social media platforms that claim they can do what they like because they are independent businesses, not public property.

Even the slightest hint of this type of tyranny must be utterly crushed in western society before it is too late and we cascade into full blown fascism in the name of liberalism. As Ronald Regan said 'If fascism ever comes to America, it will come in the name of liberalism." Like the Iron Curtain of past generations, this new Silicone Curtain has the potential to change the face of humanity and bring about the worst aspects of every science fiction book or movie ever made.

Even Bill Maher, an American, left wing talk show host, has come out and said that even though he does not like Alex Jones at all, he has the right to speak. He said, "As liberals, you are supposed to be for free speech and that means hearing things you don't agree with sometimes." And for the first time in a long time, I agree with him.

"I do not agree with what you say, but I'll defend to the death your right to say it." Evelyn Beatrice Hall.

What Can We Do?

There is no quick fix. That's the bad news. You can't just say, cancel U.N. donations, cancel all welfare and pull the military out of the war in Afghanistan (which has been raging on for 17 years now) and expect it to happen overnight. Getting things back on track is a revolution level event that we all need to agree on. So, let's get some basic stable cornerstones in place that we can all agree on first:

- **Pull on the overton window.** Work out how to discuss the more radical topics without being rude. Practice makes perfect. Ask questions rather than lecturing people. People are always interested in themselves. Start with family values and national debt with people who are more likely to be sensitive to heavier topics.

- **Start thinking as a nation.** We are a nation, not a group of smaller nations. We need to want to survive as a group. Maybe that means that we all have to change a little to meet in the middle.

- **Find common ground.** If you survey Japanese people, for example, you would get high agreement on several cultural factors. They will all like certain foods, agree on certain etiquette, agree on respect for the elderly, etc. In multicultural Australia it would take hundreds of years and multiple recessions and booms to get to the point where we all like the same food so it's never going to happen. We need to look at other areas of culture and common ground that we can all unite on.

- **Stop with the tribalism.** While it is known that smaller groups come together to form a democracy, the loyalty that a lot of people have to certain parties or communities results in stale politics and a steady march towards the greatest depression ever. We should forget all past political allegiances and consider voting for different parties every election cycle, based on current circumstances. Lab and Lib are already feeling the pinch and are cautiously leaning towards left or right accordingly in an attempt to retain a majority when poling shows that many of us are looking at alternative minority parties. Keep the pressure on by supporting minor parties and discourage socialist sympathy wherever you encounter it.

- **Be financially responsible.** It starts with us. If we have financial commonsense, we won't allow our politicians to waste our money either. The GFC should have taught a lot of people that high credit levels are dangerous and yet Aussies are still applying for low deposit home loans and interest free couches and fridges at the department store. Financial intelligence is a critical factor. Your responsible attitude toward money contributes to the nation's financial intelligence.

- **Hold media accountable.** If blatantly left wing biased, turn it off. When the mainstream media stirs up conflict or picks a side in a 50/50 topic remember they are working for a group of billionaires, with a world government agenda. They want us to argue with each other instead of uniting as one. They want us to increase national debt to give an international equalising effect. Don't let them cause us to squabble over minor issues when there is a real battle out there being fought. Turn off all left wing biased media now. Unfortunately, that's most media these days. Get out of the habit of having the news on at 6pm, don't buy the paper, don't watch the ABC or shows like The Project. If you haven't already stopped watching this crap, then try this for a month and watch yourself transform into a free thinker who questions things and forms his or her own opinions. Less propaganda in your space will change you at a spiritual level.

- **Clearly define the boundaries of democratic freedom.** When we talk about equality as a general concept it is hard to disagree. But then it evolves into hate speech laws, banning transphobia, silencing conservative media personalities and implementing racial diversity quotas in corporations and we have crossed the line into an Orwellian Dystopia that the economy and our democracy will not be able to withstand.

- **Agree that you do not want a One World Government.** Be very certain about this. This is a huge mistake and a totally unnecessary risk to take. Just imagine a scenario where someone at the top makes a bad decision or becomes corrupt and evil. Or several generations down the track a total sociopath inherits the world throne as happened to ancient Rome with Nero Caesar. Do not vote for globalist politicians under any circumstances. Even if you think the above scenario is unlikely, this type of thing is definitely possible, the fact that it is possible that some insane computation could be made in a central super government makes the risk too great. There would be no way to fight back against a one world government if it became oppressive. Thousands of years of western culture and numerous wars and revolutions have given us checks and balances, highly refined democratic structures. Magna Carta, the French revolution, the American revolution, World War 2- These history lessons have all contributed to our modern systems. We can't throw them all out the door for some unelected, left-leaning Globalist/Socialist/Monarchy/Tyranny/Oligarchy/ Technocracy.

- **Agree that the system should contain harmony and balance.** A budget deficit ten years in a row is just not ok. Any unsustainable system is not ok. It must have financial balance and sustainable freedoms that are not at risk of cascading into a full blown communist/Big Brother situation. Hate speech laws can evolve into banning Christianity and we have already seen tech bans on conservative media. This is not a well-balanced law as it can be misused and abused and can suddenly throw society into a new direction that can be directed by people in key positions.

- **Step out of your comfort zone.** Conservatives have not had to defend themselves ideologically in their own country for hundreds of years. For the bulk of us the ability to debate politics has been lost because it was unnecessary for several generations. The culture of Christianity has become more family orientated than politically active, which is good in a Christian country. It allows people to focus on their job and family. In this new climate of competing ideologies, it is necessary to sell conservatism again. Not necessarily Christianity but specifically conservatism and/or libertarianism. Prove that your view is the right choice and get good at selling it.

- **Protect freedom of speech.** Stop them from clipping our feathers. Hate speech laws are now being abused on online forums to silence political competition. These small violations on freedom of speech build up one by one until one day they will be telling us we no longer need to bother voting. Just when did it become illegal to have moderate, right wing views anyway? These hate speech laws crept in, pushed by the U.N. and they sat dormant and unenforced for decades until they were ready to strike. Then, in 2018 over the span of one month 80% of conservative voices were banned/silenced/deleted by the Tech giants claiming terms of use violations. Stating that they are private companies, so they can choose who they want to do business with. At this rate it could be illegal to speak out against the U.N. or 'urgent climate change action' soon.

- **Listen to podcasts and read books.** Supplement the lack of mainstream right wing media by reaching for it yourself. Listen while driving, mowing the lawn or whenever you can. Build on your knowledge base. It doesn't take long to find some decent sources and get up to speed.

- **View the U.N.** and any other globalist entity as a type of new religion, part of a universal ideology that is trying to push out the competition and establish power. Suddenly the zealots lose their authority when you see them for what they truly are.

- **Give yourself space to think.** Just thinking things through from start to finish, rather than looking for someone to summarise the circumstances or set the boundaries for you is the first step. If you encounter something you don't understand take a step back and think about it, before engaging in a debate with an ABC viewer. The seemingly informed leftist is often just parroting the single sided argument they heard from the media. A lifetime of propaganda from the ABC, SBS and other mainstream media sources has brainwashed many to doubt any and all conspiracy theories immediately, without thinking on it any further.

They have been implanted with the "that will never happen here" attitude which can be very hard to penetrate. They effectively have Stockholm syndrome and it takes a while to break through. The critical thought that is taught in books like George Orwell's Animal Farm and 1984 seems to have been lost over the past twenty or so years. Politics and world economics have become too complex to fully understand. So, people don't bother trying any more or they just tip toe around the subject, only becoming engaged when a politician makes a speech complaining about something or became involved in a front-page scandal.

Well, I believe there is a reason that people make certain subjects seem complex. Either they don't understand the subject themselves or they are trying to hide something from you. Economics just isn't that complex, and neither is politics. It is just like household budgeting and raising a family properly but, on a larger scale. In the old days people would read a book and then discuss it the next day. Nowadays people hit "like" on a gender inclusive meme, post a sad face emoji about illegal immigration and think that's enough politics for today.

Time and Change

Nothing remains the same forever, things are always changing, improving or decaying. Like a bicycle that is hard to balance on if it is not rolling forward. This is especially true in terms of politics. This ever-changing environment makes it all the more necessary to understand the various extreme changes that have occurred in the past so that we can influence the changes that happen in the future, rather than mindlessly walking into the same patterns over and over again. Here are some visual aids that outline my thought process when thinking of the main political structures that are possible.

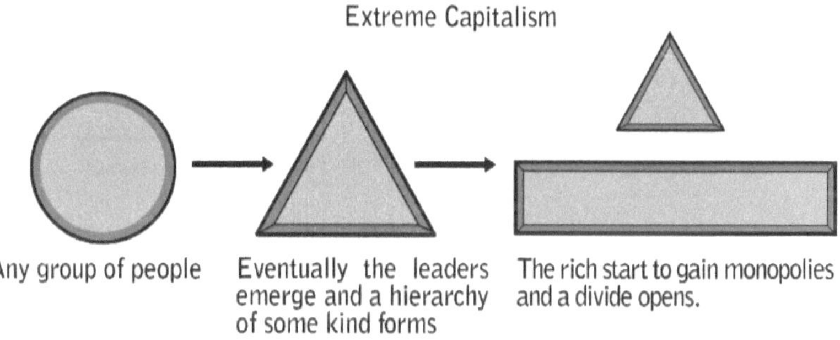

So, you start with any group of people. This is a theoretical extreme as no group starts off perfectly equally. The circle represents a lack of structure in the system. Naturally the leaders emerge, and some form of hierarchy forms which means less people with more power at the top, so it has a triangular shape. This triangular pattern is normal in almost every group of people from a company to a charity or a football team. The bosses at the top, management in the middle and everyone else at the bottom.

With extreme unrestricted capitalism we have a problem. Time favours the people at the top of the pyramid. Step by step they implement barriers to stop people from stepping up and directly competing with them. This causes a divide between the top and the rest and we end up with a structure that looks more like communism, where a small group rule the society and a gap exists between them.

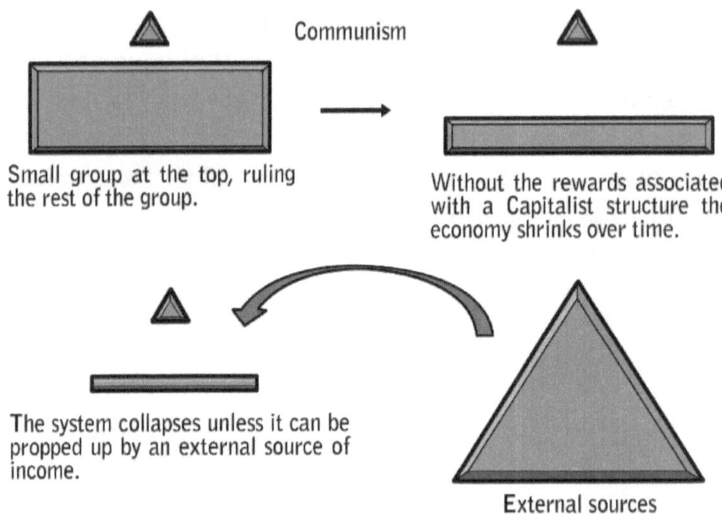

Communism, without an external source of income, will eventually shrink as an economy and therefore shrink as a population. So, it has been proven to be a weak model for long term survival when compared to other countries, if it cannot expand and swallow up others.

Cuba is a good example of a country that stopped trade with any outside nation and became stagnant and economically very poor over time. Innovation became stifled and nobody wanted to take risks. They are still producing cars to a 1950s standard even to this day. China is an example of economically successful communism. But it is dependent on other countries buying its products, so it becomes an artificially propped up system that could collapse overnight if their customers decide to shop elsewhere. So, it isn't really communism at all. It is a nation of workers forced to work in factories to serve capitalism or a version of imperialism, with an aristocratic class at the top.

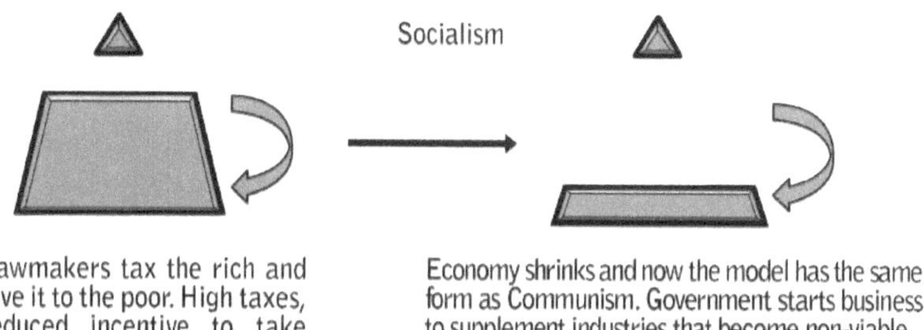

Lawmakers tax the rich and give it to the poor. High taxes, reduced incentive to take risks and be innovative.

Economy shrinks and now the model has the same form as Communism. Government starts business to supplement industries that become non-viable.

Democratic socialism is really just socialism with the word democratic thrown in front of it. The Nazi party was formed when Germany was a democracy, so the argument that it can be voted in makes no difference at all. Again, the word Nazi means Nationalist Socialist German Workers party. It is an acronym for the German words: Nationale Sozialist, they were socialists, funny how the socialists of today call the capitalists the Nazis, whilst marching around assaulting unarmed people, following in the same footsteps as the Brown Shirts. There is your short attention span and zombie level word association confusion again. The structure of democratic socialism in its late form (after an inevitable financial collapse) is the same form as socialism once you get past the basic concept of taking from the rich to give to the poor. That circular flow of energy doesn't promote production or leadership. You eventually run out of other peoples' money to tax.

It can be put on a spectrum or a scale, the more you slide down the scale the more services become government funded and so you need to take more from the rich and raise taxes and the model descends downward into a recession. The more rules you add, the more you tip the scale towards full blown socialism. The theoretical model (which has never been proven to actually work long term) would show time favouring this society, because magically everyone becomes highly ethical and works really hard (despite being given the minimum that they need to survive for free), pays enormous taxes, stays healthy and I can't even be bothered finishing that sentence.

The bottom line is, it has never worked in the long term. Venezuela is the poster child for socialism (so was Nazi Germany). The economy was booming in Venezuela in the 1970s and it drifted towards socialism and then into a more radical socialism in 1998. Now the dollar has dropped to less than 0.01% of its former value, inflation is at 13,779% and it now takes a wheelbarrow full of Bolivars to buy one US dollar.

The nation's involvement in the highly aggressive, Rockefeller run, oil industry had a part to play too. I do not believe that a nation should ever be too dependent on one market resource and a good leader would have seen this and installed safety nets to protect the economy. Safety nets like diversity of production and some support to protect a range of key industries, so that you do not become too dependent on someone else for anything. Exactly the opposite of what globalists advocate.

The Nazi party did not end with economic collapse because it was constantly growing through warfare, by seizing assets and property from other sources. It collapsed by physically losing the war but was on the verge of economic collapse because expansion had slowed down, which is why Hitler ordered the last attack across Russia in winter against all advice. A desperate move due to an unsustainable model that always runs out of resources eventually. Is Australia dependent on immigration for its economy? Do you see how the balance goes out with too much socialism?

So, looking at the above sketches, they all have a risk of leading to a model that resembles communism. These models are the flows of power and change that are true of any group of people and that includes the larger group that includes the whole world and the U.N. There are other potential models: A Monarchy, for example, literally is a group of aristocrats at the top so in a basic sketch it looks similar to communism. Fascism is just an individual dictator instead of a group at the very top. England is a constitutional monarchy, though for the purposes of my sketches it has been more like democratic capitalism for the last century or so, with a more recent leaning toward the direction of socialism with heavy welfare in place. One step at a time they have added to the government expenditure and increasing national debt with hugely expensive welfare and healthcare systems.

So, how can we overcome this? How can we have a system that isn't designed to fail. A system that isn't engineered to decline or default toward communism. Democratic capitalism is basically a capitalist model with rules and regulations in place to stop one corporation from buying or controlling everything and morphing into communism. This is what we have now, and it works fine overall, providing massive companies aren't permitted to own monopolies over things that we are all dependent on. Capitalism has brought more people out of poverty than any other system of government, which is why western countries are the ones always giving out aid, not asking for it.

Capitalism has flaws and that can be the point of discussion. The Rockefeller dynasty is a classic example of the worst case scenario, where they control monopolies over certain markets and use their power and control to start interfering with other nations at a political level, a level that should not be available to unelected businessmen. Nobody ever democratically voted them into their position. Rules should be set by democratically elected officials to ensure that business owners are not in full control over things that significantly influence society. Like, having the ability to start a world war or cause an economic depression or to delete a person's social media presence or internet-based business without breaking any serious laws.

Having said that, no system is perfect and this new movement suggesting that democratic socialism is the solution has to stop. Completely overthrowing the current system for a model of take from the rich and give to the poor is insane and unnecessary and it is guaranteed to result in problems, even if it sounds good at first. Eventually you run out of other people's money. You can have democratic capitalism and still have healthcare. Most Americans on the left think they need to completely overthrow capitalism in order to have government funded healthcare.

Personally, I'd rather have a job and the right to select my own healthcare fund than be unemployed and have everyone forced into an inefficient, government run program. Maybe they could afford it once their national debt is brought down by twenty trillion dollars or so. But even then, the argument against it is strong. The most important thing, more important than healthcare, is that the system has longevity. It must be sustainable otherwise the bubble will burst. National debt is the key factor to indicate when democratic capitalism is tilting too far left. It is the simplest, quickest way to glance at the overall scene and get an indication of whether the direction is good or bad and that information is readily available to everyone. It shows, quite simply, whether or not you can afford the things that you want as a society. An engaged public with the ability to have their say and listen to other opinions is the only way to keep it working long term.

Thank you for reading my book. I hope it has given you some things to think about and some tools to think with, that you may not have had before now. At least if you're thinking about your country, you are doing better than some. Too many people are not engaged in politics and society and think that is a job for the experts. Many people are lead around by whatever gossip the newspaper is talking about today.

Well, maybe the small print in a Bill in the House of Commons requires some expertise; but having an overview of the scene and direction is certainly our job and it is not that hard to have an opinion on the basics. The final chapter will help you to discuss the important topics that are politically charged, without being spat on by a communist. It is a subtle art form but one we must work on if we are going to get our message out.

Where to now?

Debating

The final chapter is about discussing this subject with others. In marketing the term sound bite is used to describe the short, sharp and highly effective advertising phrases used in brochures, ads, sales presentations, etc. The same can be said of politics. If you can condense your viewpoint into short sharp sentences, then the listener is more likely to:

A) Hear you,
B) Understand what you have said; and
C) Pass it on.

Memes are similar in social media but not so useful in good old-fashioned verbal conversation. The 'sound bite' gets in quick before their attention span runs out but has the bonus effect of being easy to remember and therefore easier to use when put on the spot. "Freedom of speech is fragile", "The debt bubble will burst". These kind of statements must be tested on people in conversation and committed to memory.

It is how we need to speak nowadays to keep people's attention long enough to get your point across. People will start to talk over you if you stutter, sound unsure or pause too long to think of the correct wording. Also, people will outright stop listening if you are too extreme with conspiracy theories or start lecturing them, making it difficult for them to chime in with their opinions. So, it is advisable to initially stick to the topics that they can agree on and hold off on the heavier stuff or the minor details until after they have agreed with some of the basic commonsense building block elements of your argument first. Don't dump all of your knowledge on them in one heavy conversation.

You need to be able to say each point in one breath, because that is all the time many will give you. I advise people to prepare for political conversations by predicting the top ten or so hot social/

political subjects and having one or two sound bites ready to go for when you are challenged or put on the spot. Get in the habit of bursting out your message in three or four words. This grabs attention and if you do it right, you are then permitted more time to elaborate. Opinion leaders debate topics on the radio and in podcasts, etc.

If you search hard and find some good ones, listen closely to them and they will give you the sound bites to use in your own conversations. This is half of the reason they are censoring them in social media. They will often say the same message in a few different ways to make sure it gets through. That is the importance of these leaders and they are the first ones to be targeted in an information war. Actually, this shortage of high quality, right wing representation in the mainstream media is the entire problem. Staunch Liberal voters are still watching the ABC.

There are different levels of debate that can be employed. The foaming at the mouth lefty will often employ the bottom two levels of Paul Graham's Hierarchy of Disagreement. The higher you are on this chart, the more intelligent the level of conversation and the more likely you are to win a debate. Contradictory to this, you will often need to use a sound bite first in order to get their attention, so they grant you time to explain your point further. The lower levels include name calling and discrediting the other person, rather than directly responding to what has been said. This is called argumentum ad hominem and this is the highest level of debate the mainstream left will bring to most debates. Bigot, racist, climate change denier, fascist, don't believe this guy because he also said such and such, just look at his Facebook profile, etc...

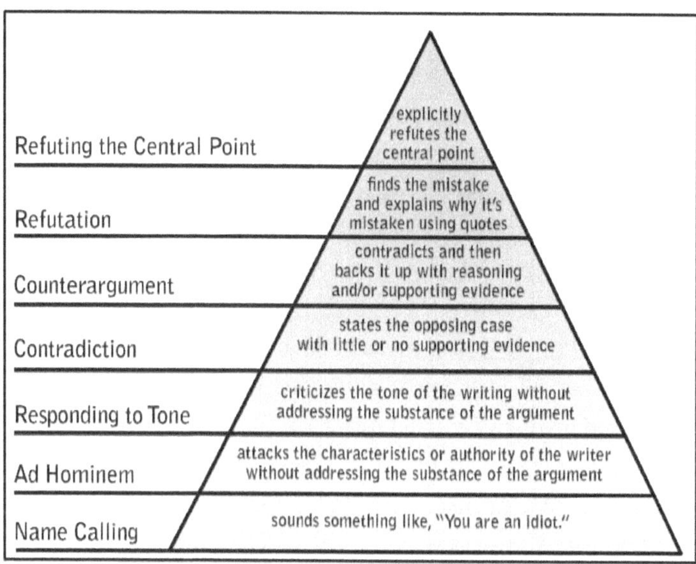

Paul Graham's Hierarchy of Disagreement lists ad hominem as the second lowest type of argument in a disagreement.

Ad Hominem arguments have their place too, the meme wars have united the right through Facebook, which is why memes have now been banned in the EU under copyright law. President Trump is the master of name calling. It is effective but you must be able to follow up with higher level conversation after initially getting their attention.

Many moderate right wingers are atheists. This puts a barrier up where they feel they cannot support certain candidates that they do not fully identify with, such as Christians. This barrier needs to be broken down so that people can look at the candidate's individual policies, rather than taking one factor they disagree with and then ceasing to listen to that person from then on, as if we were all voting once for a lifetime president or senator.

It is important to discuss individual topics and policies at the higher levels of the hierarchy of disagreement to differentiate between ineffective chit chat and effective, productive debate. The idea that you have to vote for the same party every time there is an election needs to be broken, to get through the tribalism and loyalties that have given us such stagnant politics for 20 years and allowed the Liberal Party to drift left.

Form a squad, a band of brothers that you know will agree with you on at least some of the main items in this book. Engage with them first, to practice your political conversation and sharpen your quick high-level answers. Talk to them regularly about politics and social issues. Hold off on talking to the type of people who think Obama was the greatest president, until you really know what you're talking about. The way the alt left generally debate is by undermining your certainty and mocking you, like high school bullies. They discredit your sources and try to make you look stupid before you realise they don't really know anything themselves.

They want to prove that your news source is wrong. If they can prove that you are a little unsure, it reinforces that their "official" source material is the best. Instead of thinking about it and working this out themselves, they are just seeing you as a competing source of information and testing you for weakness before they even consider accepting you as their new master. They have too much riding on you being wrong to actually start thinking about things like economics. They are firmly on the left. The left has its place in a two-party-preferred system so, don't even bother to try to get them to change sides.

The sleeping right wingers, not the alt right, the "just right" are the ones who have the power to get us back us on track and restore balance. These are the comatose apex predators, the Wedge-tailed eagles that have had their wings clipped for too long. This is where the true power which can restore balance lies dormant.

Team up with a squad, supplement your moderate right wing media with podcasts and alternative books to earn your wings and you will eat the little bunny rabbits on the left for breakfast and wake up your dormant right wing friends at the same time. Take two minutes right now to list nine people that you could regularly agree with on general social topics and politics. Some who know more than you and others who need to learn a bit more. Don't censor your list at all, just throw the nine names down on paper. You must list all nine in the next two minutes to avoid subconsciously screening the list too much. Go!

Now cross out any far leftists. There could be a couple on there. Now cross out the uneducated centrists too. These are the ones that think they are educated when they just parrot the mainstream ABC narratives. Every discussion turns into an argument or they just go silent and awkward. Just leave them out of the group all together. It is easier to leave them out now than evict them later. You are forming your core training squad and the group is not meant to have just anyone as members.

Now that you have a base list, the next step is to get them all on the program. You could start a Facebook closed group page with patriotism as the general topic or just catch up socially. Whatever floats your boat. Caution against steering too far right wing and encouraging the group to one up each other by being racist dickheads or going too far in to amusing each other with gay jokes. This isn't about being an actual far right group and belittling people or being ignorant, it is about educating each other on the basic principles of our democracy, exchanging ideas, learning, practicing discussing politics and keeping each other informed. Keep it light to start with, maybe introduce them to this book to see if they are interested in the purpose of the group.

Practice discussing politics without being too politically incorrect, so that you can use those skills in other groups. This is the basic reason that the right wing has let itself be clipped. The right wing has just taken a bit longer to adapt to the modern PC rules. If you think about it, you can probably get by fine without telling a transsexual joke. People who aren't interested in politics need to be introduced to the subject, otherwise they default to the mainstream media narrative, which is much more left-leaning than right. I'd rather censor myself a little bit and get the message of patriotism out, than not get the message out and lose my country.

Talk about the podcasts you listen to, ask them what they listen to. I listen to mine while mowing the lawn or driving in my car. Not everyone has unlimited time to listen to them all, so talk instead and share what you've learned in short "sound bites". What political books have you read lately that were worth a read? This type of thing. Practice the art of talking about politics politely and using sound bites and catch phrases that quickly summarize a position. Make note of whether people are laughing or engaging, or are they looking bored? This is training for the real game!

Represent the real right wing, the wing with economic viability and personal safety at heart. The family man who works hard and isn't afraid to point out a problem when he sees one. Don't be baited into identifying as a racist or a bigot. That isn't you, that is how the left paint you. The idea is to supplement and build up the type of patriotic, nationalist media that has been stifled and defunded in this country and connect your friends to it too.

Friends don't let friends watch the ABC. Real news is out there, it is just slightly harder to find than what is forced on to us by the left. Build up your sources yourself, rather than being lazy and watching the free to air leftist owned TV, newspaper and radio. Many of these guys are keen to learn but have not taken the time to do their own research, so when "The Project" is on in the back ground, this is the only message that gets in under the radar.

As I said earlier in the book, many of these guys have lefty family members so they don't "like" or "follow" things on Facebook that could trigger their unemployed, single SJW sister in law. This prevents them from following certain pages or exploring the topic and learning more. Once you have established a base and are armed to the teeth with good arguments by drilling and ironing out your thoughts with your squad members in a closed group setting, you can move out from a position of strength and tackle the next social tier with confidence.

It really doesn't take much to be far more informed than the mainstream subscribing types. The right sources will give you the right viewpoint on current topics. Once you are confident it is your patriotic duty to spread the word. Start a YouTube channel, write your own book or blog. If just ten people see a three minute video, you have communicated with ten other people. Imagine speaking with ten individual people giving you their undivided attention for three minutes each. Even just a few views makes it worthwhile.

Rather than approaching a sensitive topic bluntly, change the paradigm, taking it one step higher and steer the conversation towards protecting freedom of speech and particularly political speech. There is no need to jump straight into a street fight with a psychotic communist. Under this strategy you may be relieved to find that it is never necessary to even speak to them. They will always be far left and are not the key to balancing our society. Take the easy road instead. We only need to wake up enough people to balance the scales.

The first target outside of your immediate training squad is the Liberal Party voter who still watches leftist mainstream media, like the ABC or reads the newspaper every morning. The guy who should be right wing but finds himself so saturated in left wing material that he isn't sure and votes for the Liberal Party regardless of how far left it shifts. The guy (or girl) who is following the globalist left agenda without questioning anything. Maybe someone who runs a small business or is self-employed, so can't in good conscience vote Labor. But then acts like a dead cat when you raise political subjects and says something like "Life is pretty good here, we have nothing to complain about. There's always going to be someone trying to take over the world".

This is the centrist, the sleeping right winger that needs to be awoken. This is the guy that has been sat on the bench for thirty years and has allowed the Liberal party to shift so far left, it is almost where Labor used to be. We need to batter them with organised, informed debate and chip away at their media sources to re-establish credible, right wing media.

Discredit and disconnect him from the left-leaning material that is crossing into our air space and connect him with anti-globalist, right wing alternatives for his daily injection of politics. Make the effort to rebalance the scale. Balance, that is all that is required. You don't need to convert everyone into thinking exactly the same as you.

The great paradox of democratic culture is this:
We must polarise to unite.
Disagree to achieve harmony.

It is such an amazing conflict. To become even close to a uniform culture we need to protect the right to argue and debate. This requires free speech and room to move and make mistakes. We need both a right and left wing!

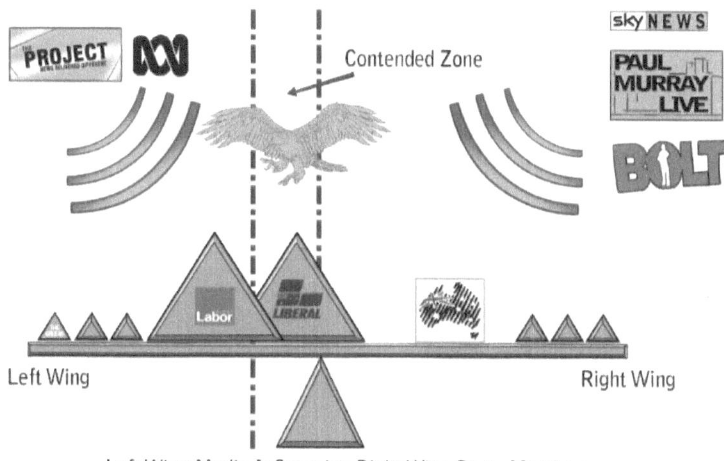

Left Wing Media Influencing Right Wing Party Members
Eagle Protecting Contended Zone

This idea that we can all meet in the middle under a grown-up centrally owned, progressive media and agree on all social issues nearly gave us a one-party state, which is basically on the path to communism. The violation of the two-wing system is a far greater enemy than the left wing will ever be. The left has its place, imagine a far right government like Saudi Arabia where you can be executed for practicing sorcery or speaking out against Islam.

We need open debate left and right and a two-wing, democratic system to remain balanced. Not a central new world government with a socialist doctrine with no democratic checks and balances. Know that free speech, both left and right is always going to be under attack by someone.

There is always some way that they will justify it and we may even agree with aspects of the argument at first.

We must stop it as soon as we encounter it and insist that they work out their issues some other way. The two-party-preferred system is worth keeping and that requires open freedom of speech on both sides to work properly. Celebrate our right to debate freely, instead of feeling bad that people don't always agree. I have lost all respect for the far left, but there is a place for the Labor voter in our country. If we can take out the globalist narratives and get people back on the patriotic side of the line, we will restore the natural balance of the two-party-preferred system.

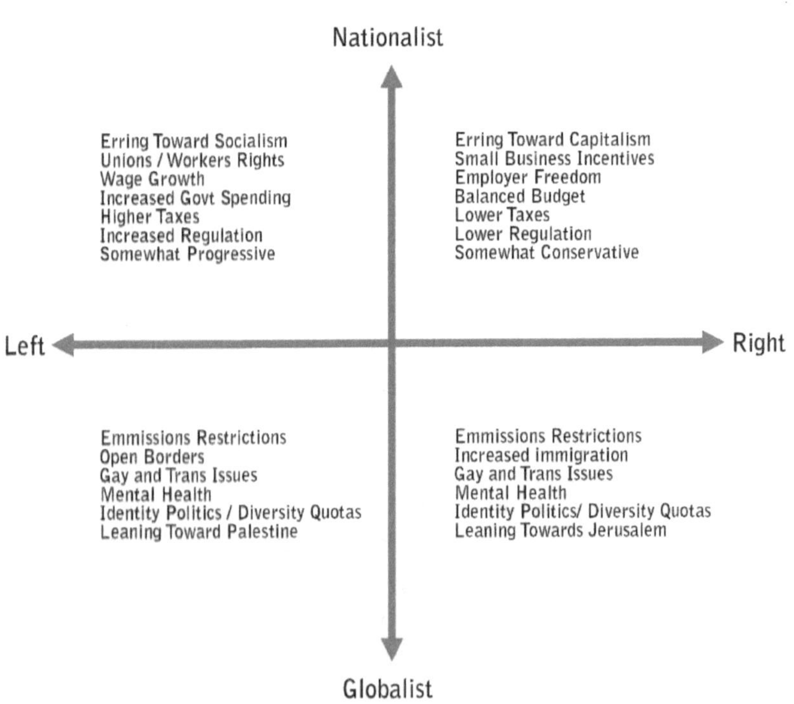

Disagreement and open debate is at the core of western culture, as it keeps us moving forward rather than being heavily stuck in tradition and obedience to government like so many other cultures. The root of our clipped feathers is the hate speech laws and social media regulations that need to be revised. We must grit our teeth and learn to work within the current rules to get our message out and then change the laws back to allow for full freedom of speech.

Freedom of political speech is supposed to be constitutionally protected but it is being attacked on all fronts. Without fair debate we simply don't get all angles of a topic and that restriction is a mind control technique that is being used against all of us.

Freedom of political speech must be maintained to ensure that we have full access to a diverse range of opinion leaders in our community. If you have nothing more to do with politics in your entire lifetime but you absolutely, unreservedly insist on our right to have unrestricted political freedom of speech, then your contribution to politics will have been significant.

See you on the battlefield.

Peaceful Dove

It could not fly.
It could just sing.
Nature was not kind
To the bird with one wing.

What good is a bird
that cannot fly?
How does it survive?
One wonders why.

Move over mate
So sorry I'm late.
Let me show you now
what it is to be great.

Let me balance the scale
before we all fail.
If we all have a say
Maybe truth will unveil.

Oh, that poor little dove
with just one wing.
It could not fly.
It could just sing.

Tell us what you think:

Visit our Facebook page "Clipped Wing" and get involved.

Or, if Zuckerberg deletes our page try our backup page:
"Clipped Wing 2"